CHEECH AND CHONG...

are just two nice, normal guys
trying to stay alive in the big city—
and dealing with such heavy social issues as:
a TV career at Copycat Productions,
their nosey neighbor Mr. Neatnick,
and true love in the Welfare line.

Can they manage to rise above it in the end?
That's all in a day's unemployment in
CHEECH AND CHONG'S NEXT MOVIE

CHEECH AND CHONG
in
"CHEECH AND CHONG'S NEXT MOVIE"
Written by THOMAS CHONG
& CHEECH MARIN
Associate Producer PETER MACGREGOR-SCOTT
Produced by HOWARD BROWN
Directed by THOMAS CHONG
A Universal Picture

Cheech and Chong's Next Movie

© 1980 UNIVERSAL CITY STUDIOS, INC. ALL RIGHTS RESERVED.

BY THOMAS CHONG & CHEECH MARIN

DESIGNED BY TOM NOZKOWSKI

A JOVE BOOK

Copyright © 1980
by MCA Publishing,
a Division of MCA Inc.
All rights reserved.

All rights reserved. No part of this publication may be reproduced or transmitted in any form or by any means, electronic or mechanical, including photocopy, recording, or any information storage and retrieval system, without permission in writing from the publisher.

*Requests for permission to make copies of any part of the work should be mailed to:
MCA Publishing, 100 Universal City Plaza,
Universal City, California 91608*

First Jove edition published July 1980

10 9 8 7 6 5 4 3 2 1

Printed in the United States of America

Jove books are published by Jove Publications, Inc.,
200 Madison Avenue
New York, N.Y. 10016

Cheech and Chong are two lovable, upright guys, just trying to get along in the big city. Do they make it? That's what this book is all about. . . .

                  Read on

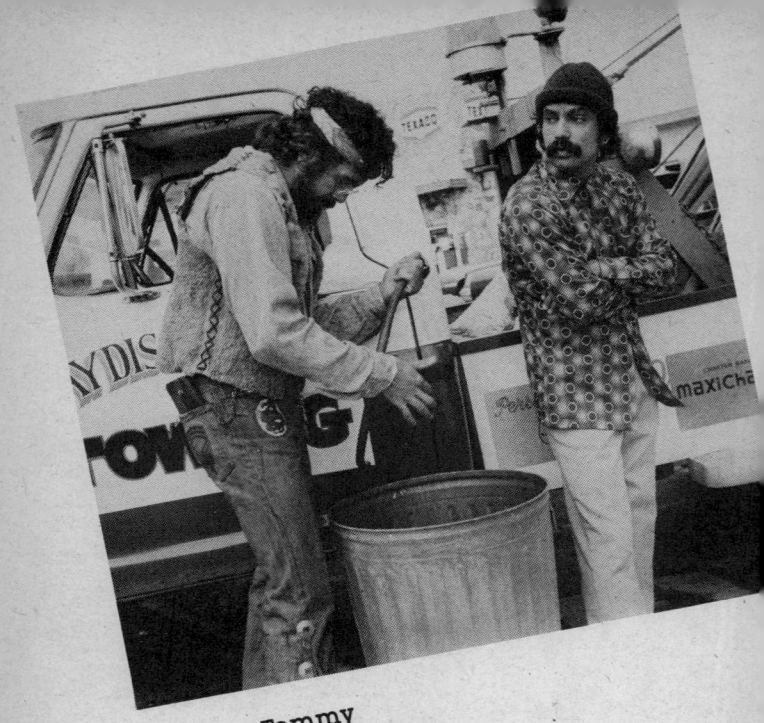

Tommy
This is the pits!

Cheech
Just be cool, man. Nobody's lookin' at you.

Tommy
We need a funnel.... Don't spill it. Watch out!

Cheech
That's smelly gasoline.... Careful, I gotta go to work in these clothes!

Meanwhile, at Copycat Productions, work has begun on a TV movie. For the 47th time the director is trying to get the three female leads to act scared.

Cheech arrives at work straight from the explosion hoping to con Kim, the wardrobe mistress, into getting him clean clothes. He turns on the charm.

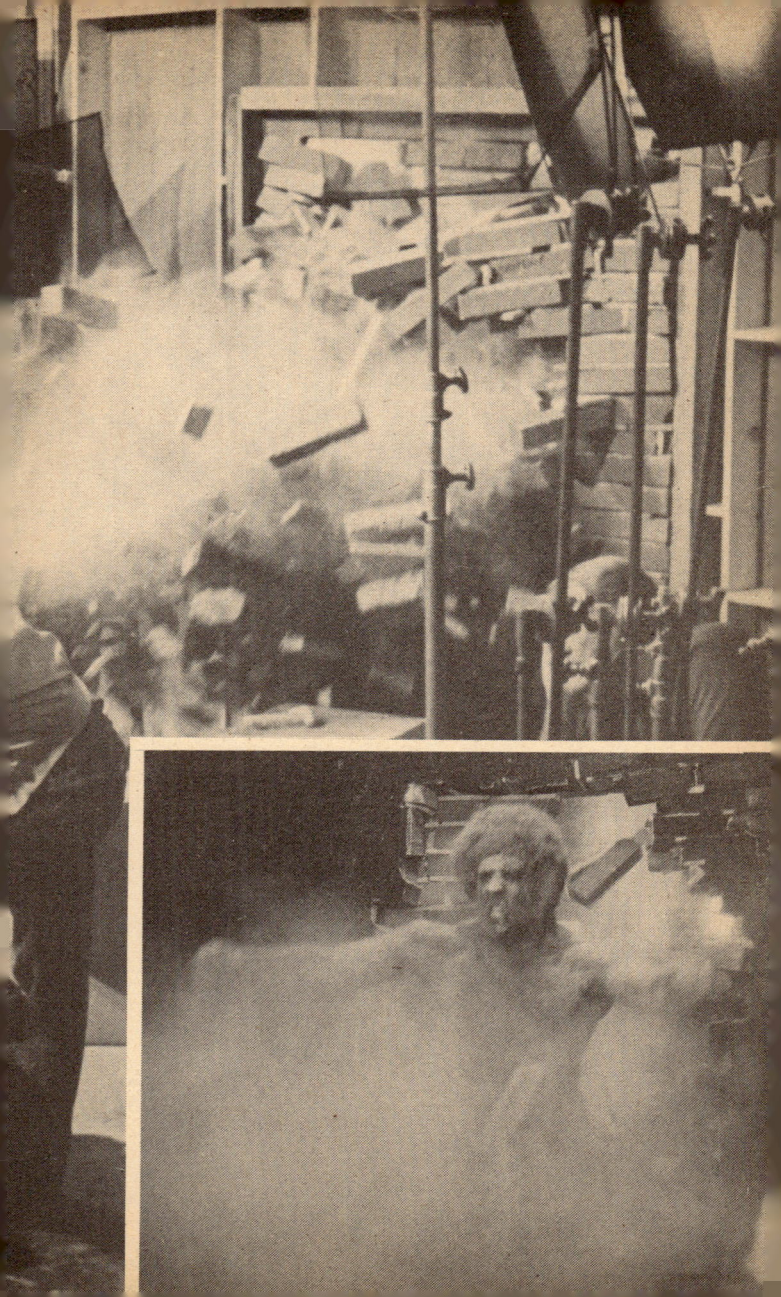

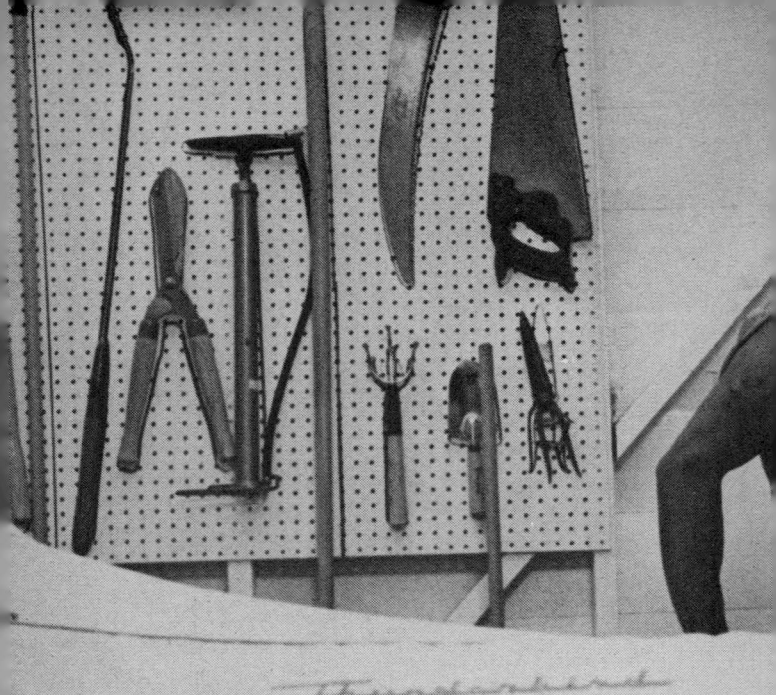

Back in the neighborhood Tommy Chong slips the borrowed T-Bird back under its cover.

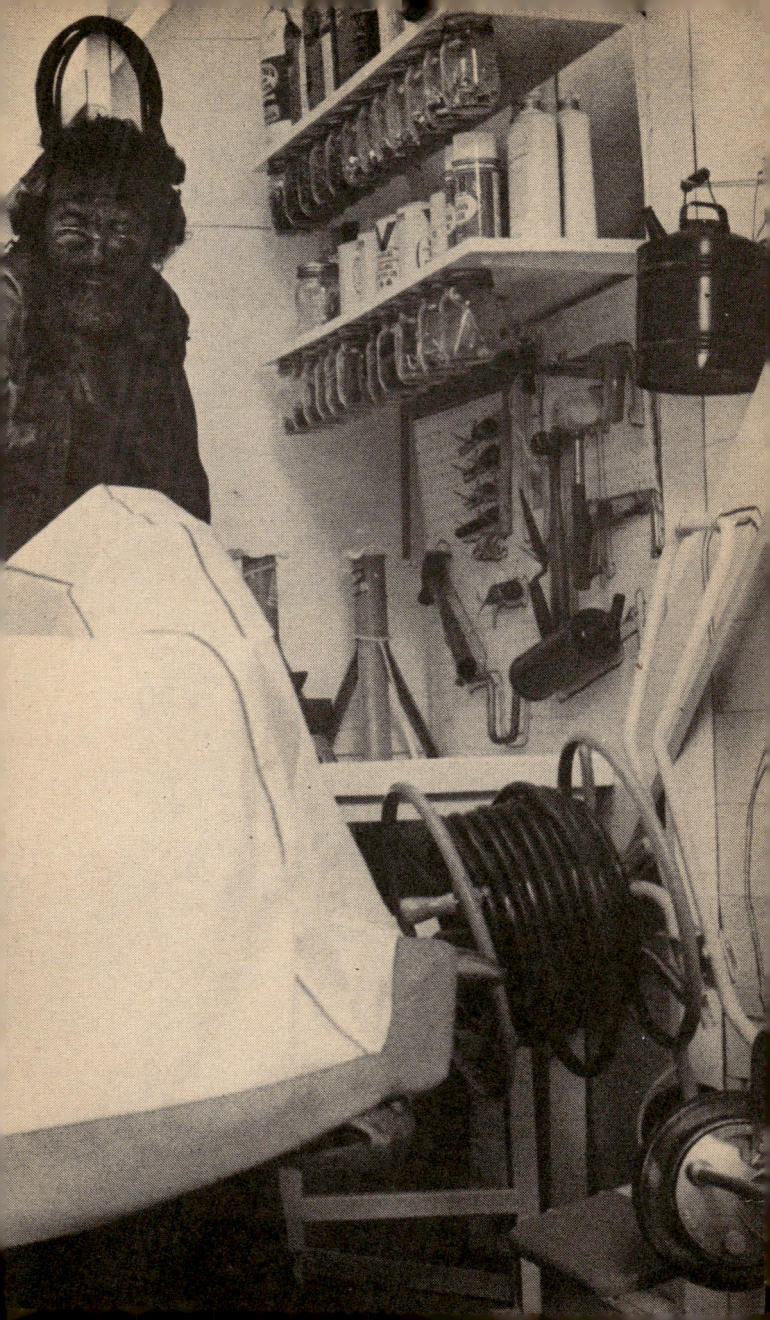

Mr. Neatnick

This is Mr. Neatnick, at war with the neighborhood, especially the boys next door — Cheech and Chong. Neatnick knows they're always up to no good.

A friendly neighborhood chat across the back fence.

After a hard day, there's nothing like a relaxing motorcycle ride . . .

VRRRRRRRRRRROOM!
VRRRRRRRRRRRROOM!

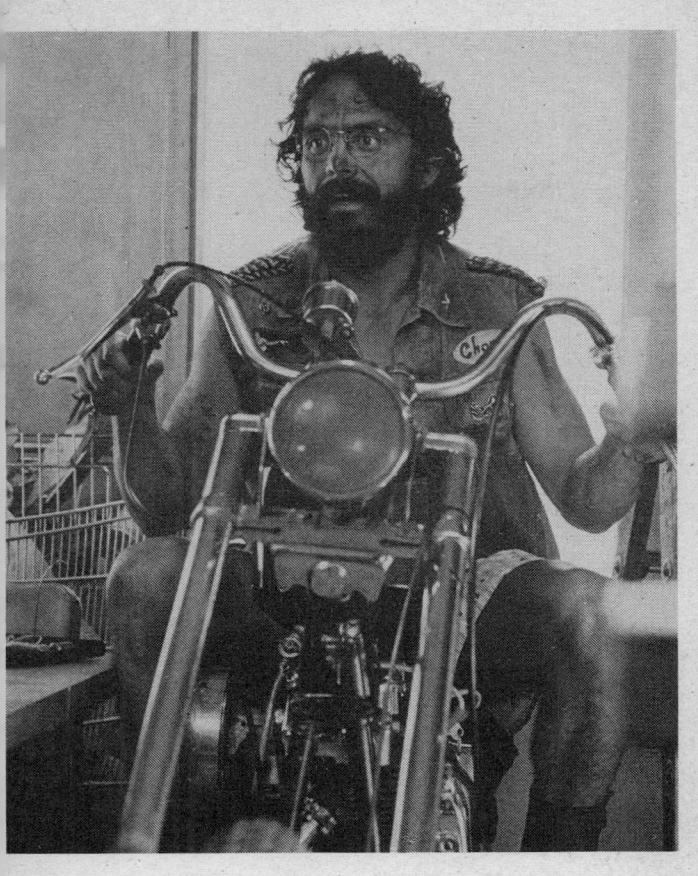

. . . in the comfort of your own kitchen.

After his nice bike ride, Tommy puts in his earplugs and plays a serenade.

. . . and on . . . and on . . . and on . . . and on!

Cheech tears Tommy away from his music.

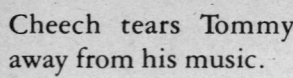

Man, wait 'til you see what I've got in the van.

And then, Neatnick spies the loot.

Nosey Neatnick knows a good piece of junk when he sees it.

Listen fellas, if I can have Greta Garbo's tutu and this other stuff, I won't turn you in.

WHEN YOU GO TO THE BARRIO IN A BORROWE[D]

VAN, IT'S ALWAYS BEST TO CUSTOMIZE IT FIRST.

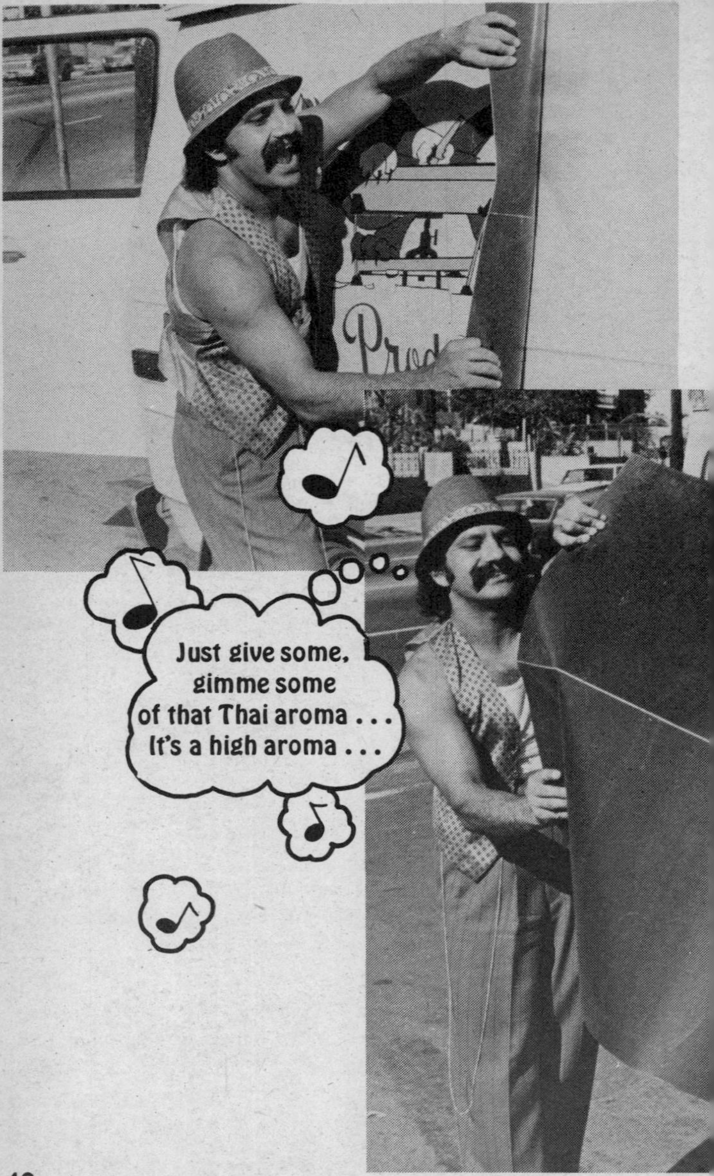
Just give some,
gimme some
of that Thai aroma . . .
It's a high aroma . . .

When customizing, it helps if you can just peel back the Studio logo on the side panel to reveal an appropriately heroic Aztec mural.

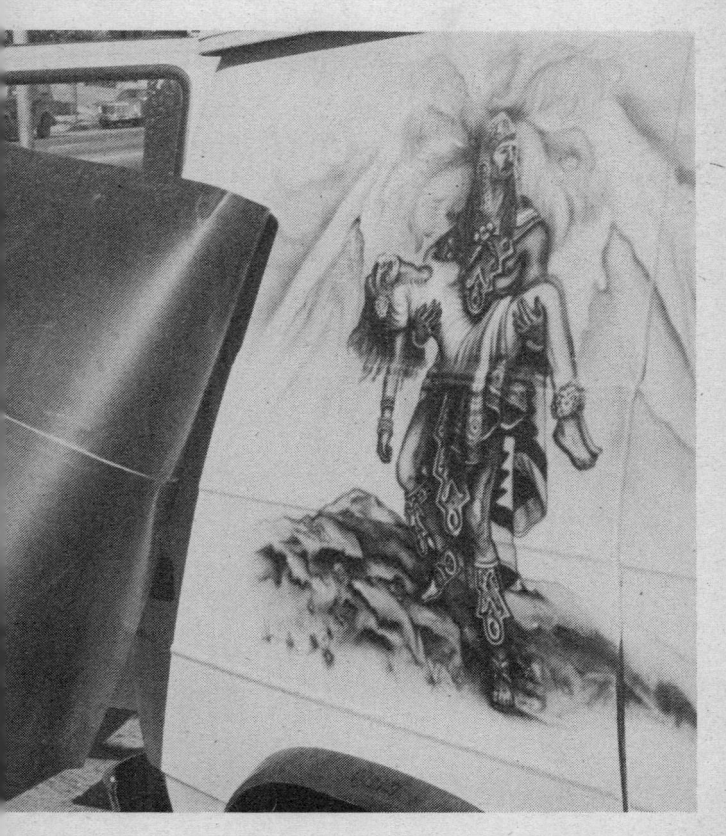

42

Back in the neighborhood, it's a dog's life.

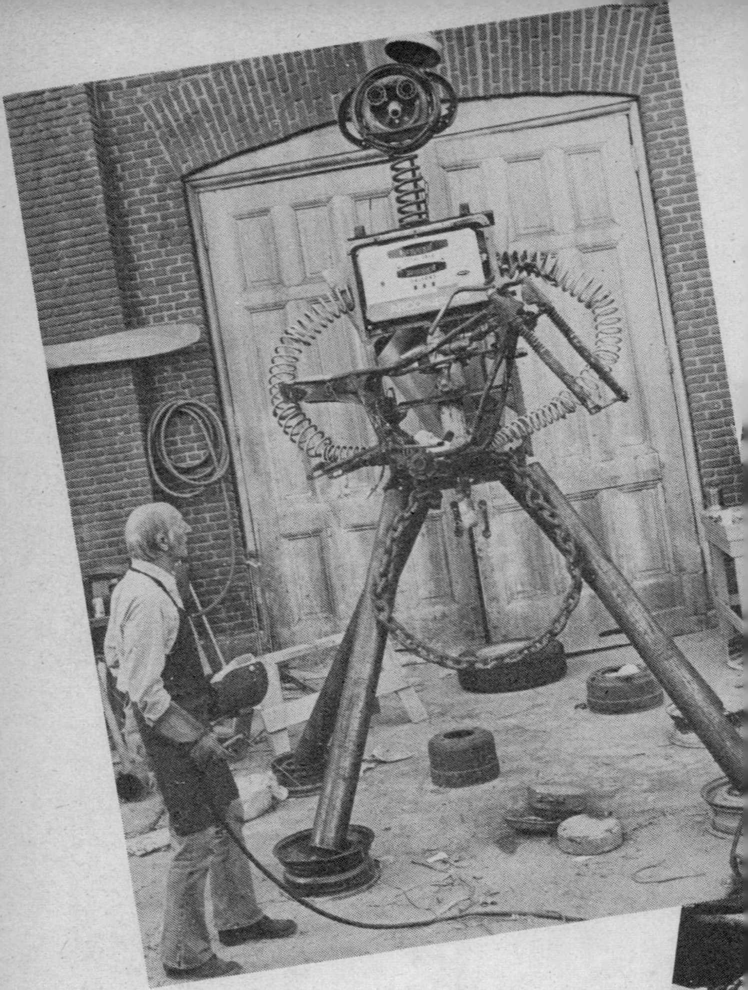

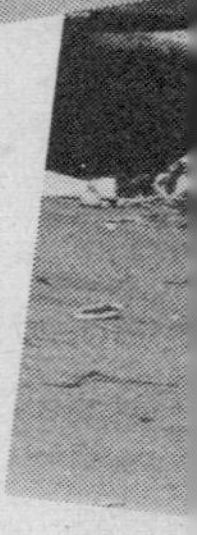

THE STREET SCENE

Left: A local sculptor and his latest creation.

Below: The corner wino trades in his old garbage for a fresh supply.

The next morning · · ·

... Tommy freshens up at the goldfish tank.

> You took the van?
> Man,
> I was gonna return it. . . .

Cheech gets a call from the studio.

You mean I'm fired!
TMENT OF PUBLIC SOC
PLEASE DO NOT GET IN LINE UNTIL YOUR REPORT TIME
4
5

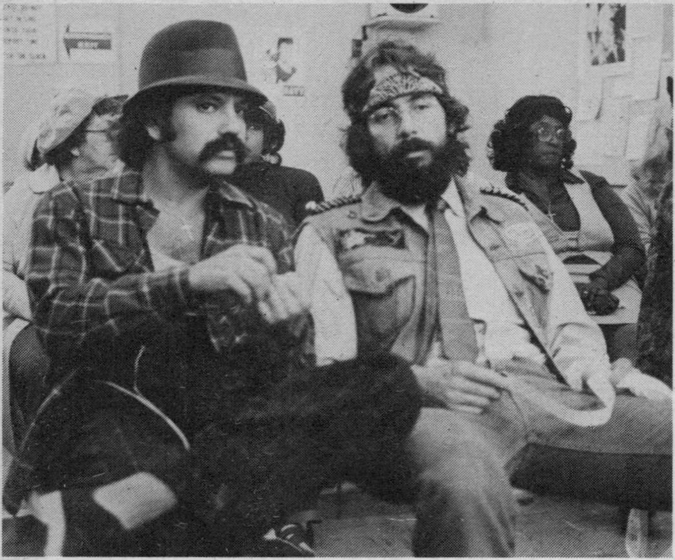

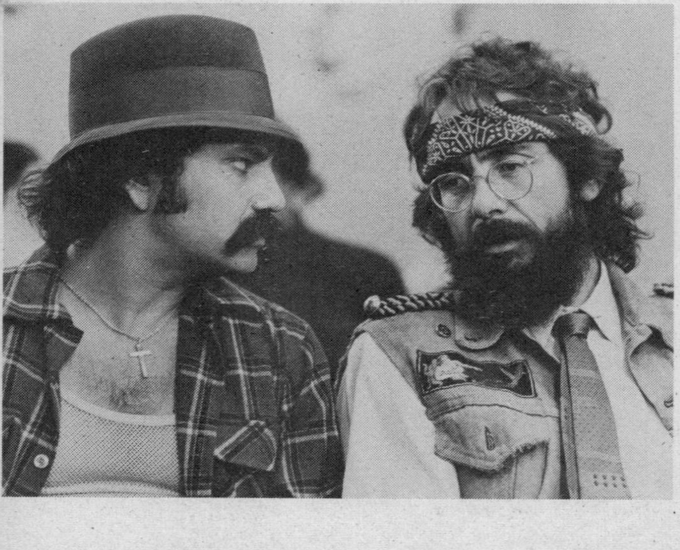

Cheech
OK, now let's rehearse.
He says, "How many dependents do you have?"

Tommy
Two.

Cheech
Not two. Twenty.
You got that? Twenty.

Tommy
Yeah, twenty — like you have
ten and I have ten.

Cheech
OK, now what else you gonna say?

Tommy
Gimme the money.

Cheech
No, no, no. You say, "I've looked
for employment three times this
week and have not found any."
And if they get rough with you,
just say, "Look, if I knew you were
going to hassle me, I would've
gone to a teen center."

LOVE BLOOMS IN

Sweet Donna,
Cheech's girl friend.

...E WELFARE OFFICE

Cheech, in a serious moment, considers how best to catch the attention of the girl of his dreams. . . . Perhaps a bouquet of flowers, a box of candy, or . . .

. . . a funny face and loud noises.

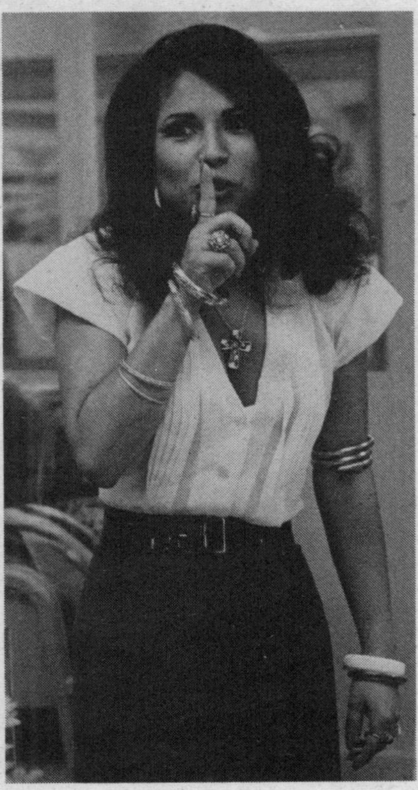

Donna
Come to the back room, baby!

Cheech
(thinking)
Ah'm so fine.

Tommy
(to himself)
It worked!!!

The young lovers share a private moment. That manic-looking fellow in the foreground is the notorious Man of a Thousand Noises; he's getting ready to do his thing. . . .

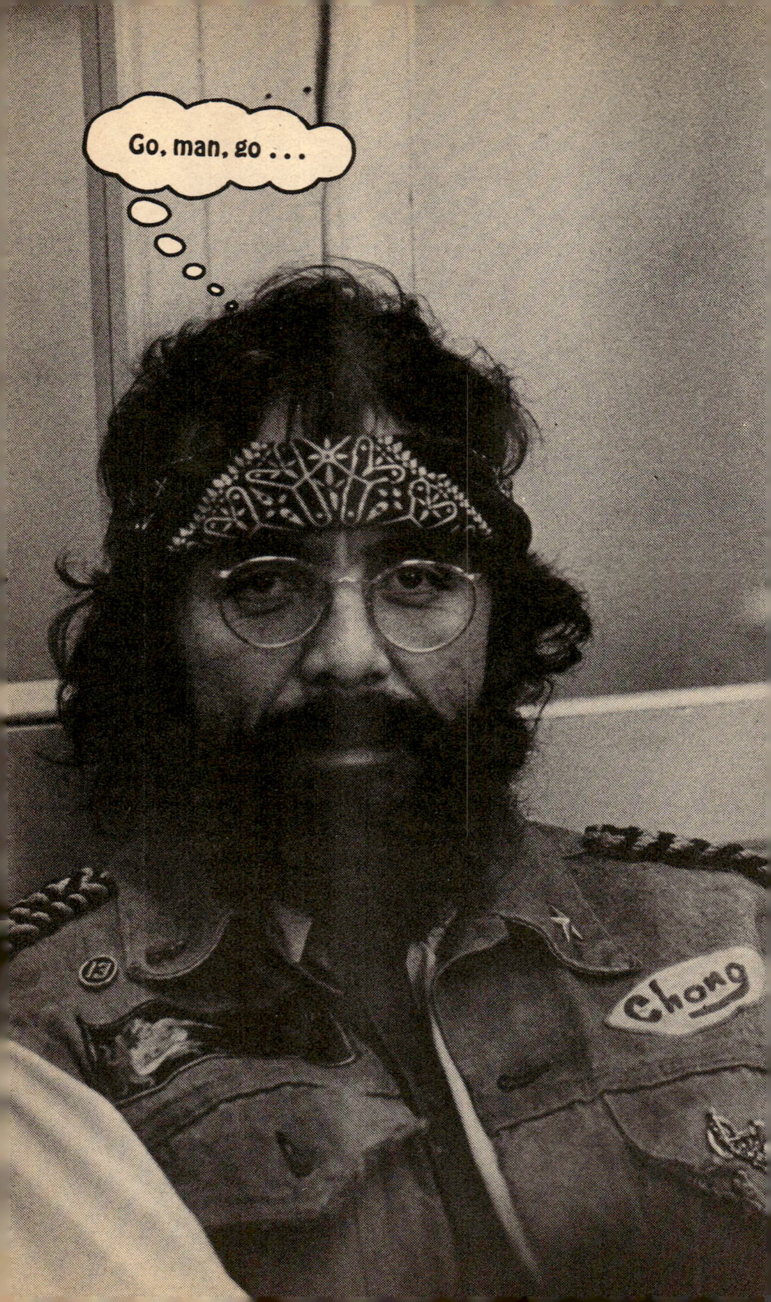
Go, man, go . . .
Chong

Whooo—Whoooo!
Breet—Tweet—Phweet!
ZZZOOOM!   Toot—Toot!
Chugga—Chugga . . .

Bleep-bloop-blap
Choo–Choo

Tommy, a connoisseur of music, and the wino seated to his right, who also has heard some funny sounds in his time, are just the folks to appreciate this human noisemaker. . . .

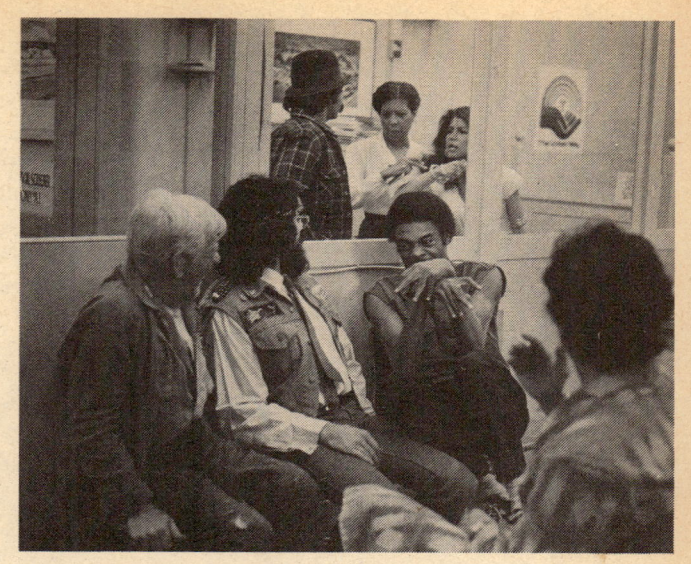

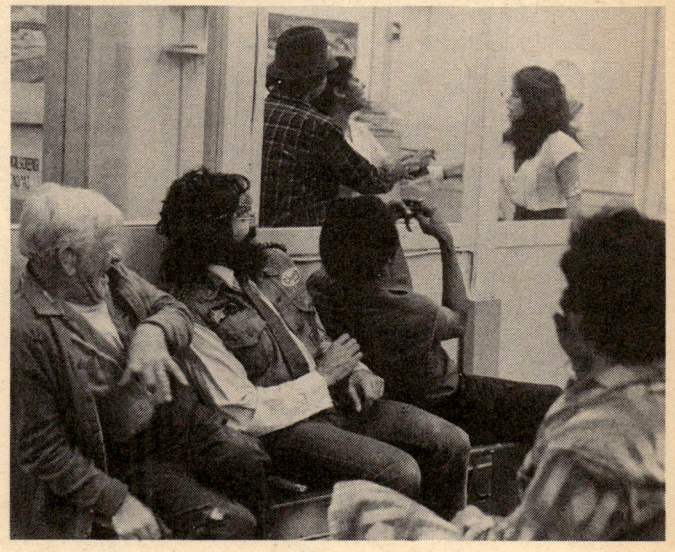

The welfare supervisor discovers Cheech and Donna. Now, pandemonium *really* breaks out!

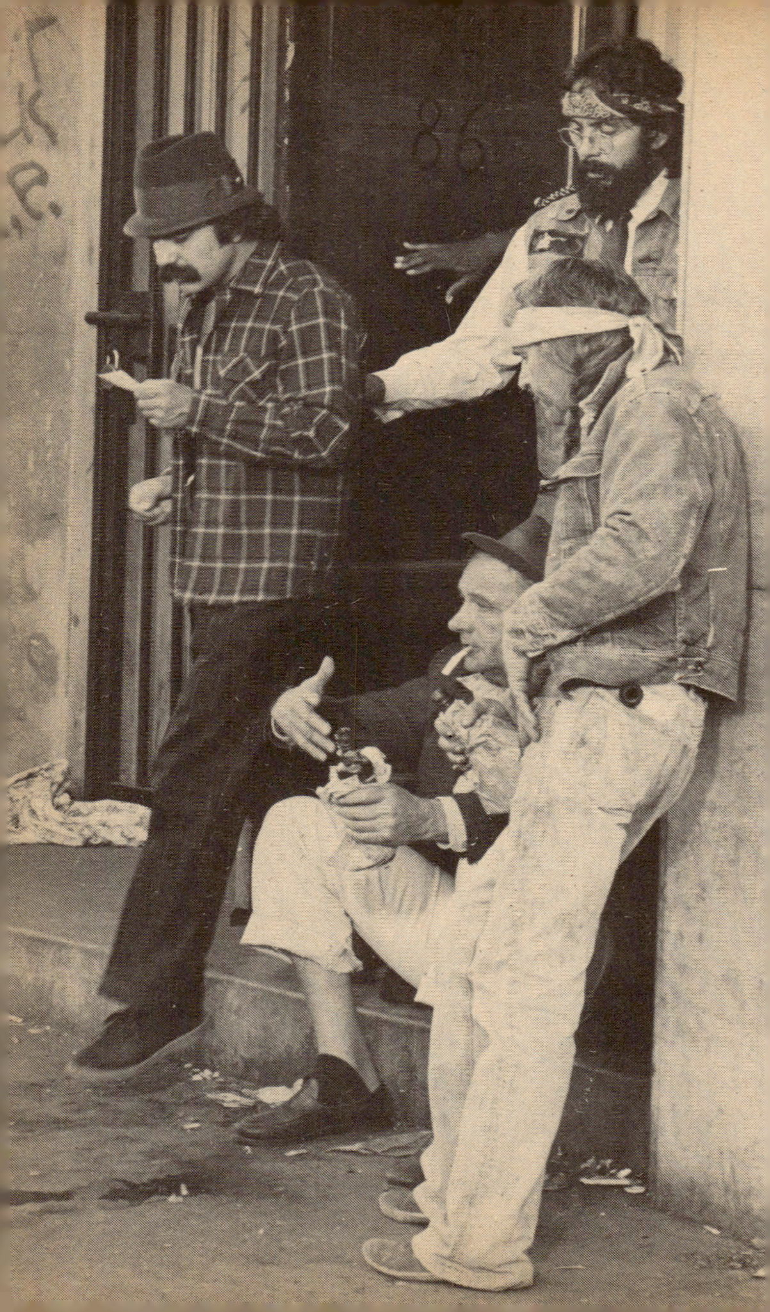

Donna's supervisor sends Cheech and Tommy to Door 86 for special attention. . . . They find themselves in the back alley.

Cheech doesn't care that they got the bum's rush. . . . He's got a date tonight with the Fair Donna.

Where's Dave?

Dave's not here

...TING ...ADED ...NE

> Cousin Red! Tonight... oh man... not tonight. I got a date with Donna. Tommy will take care of you.

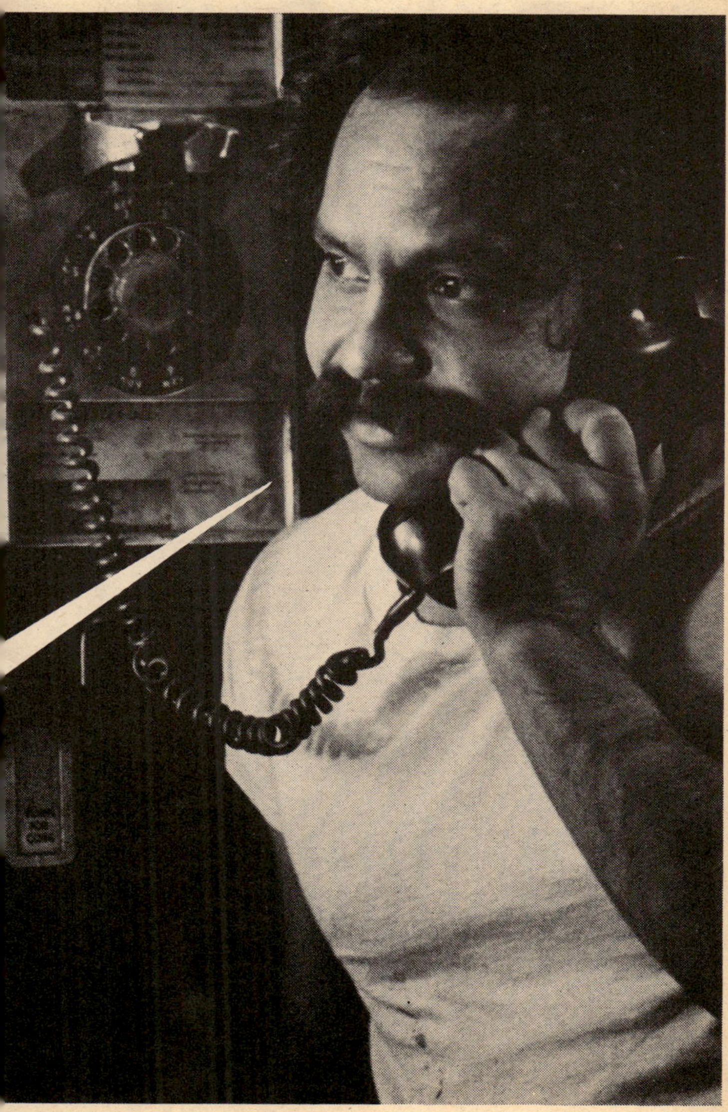

Anticipating Donna's reaction to his taste in art, Cheech covers up the evidence.

Cheech practices his moves for the big date.

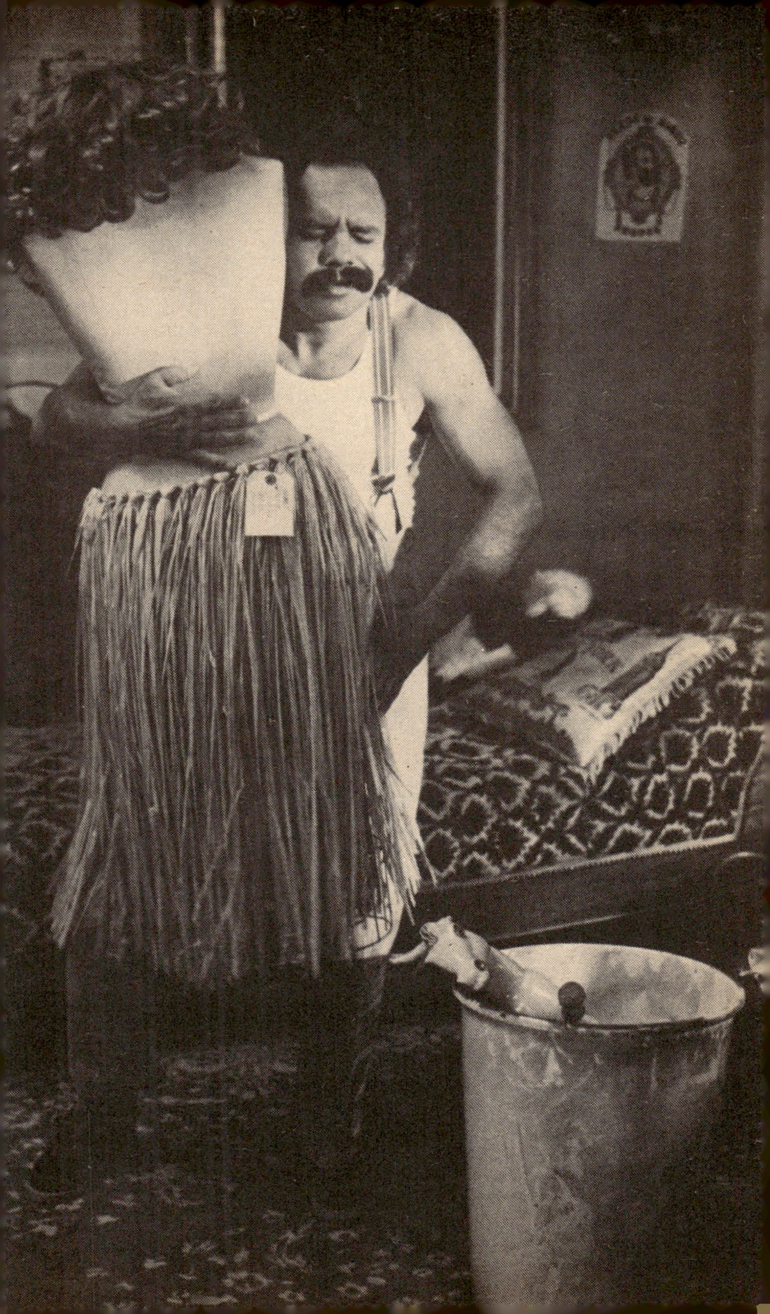

Cousin Red

This is Cheech's country cousin (see the family resemblance?), a simple farm boy until that fateful day when someone planted strange seeds on his property. When Red discovered cows with smiles on their faces, he tried the funny weed, and now he, too, always has a smile on his face.

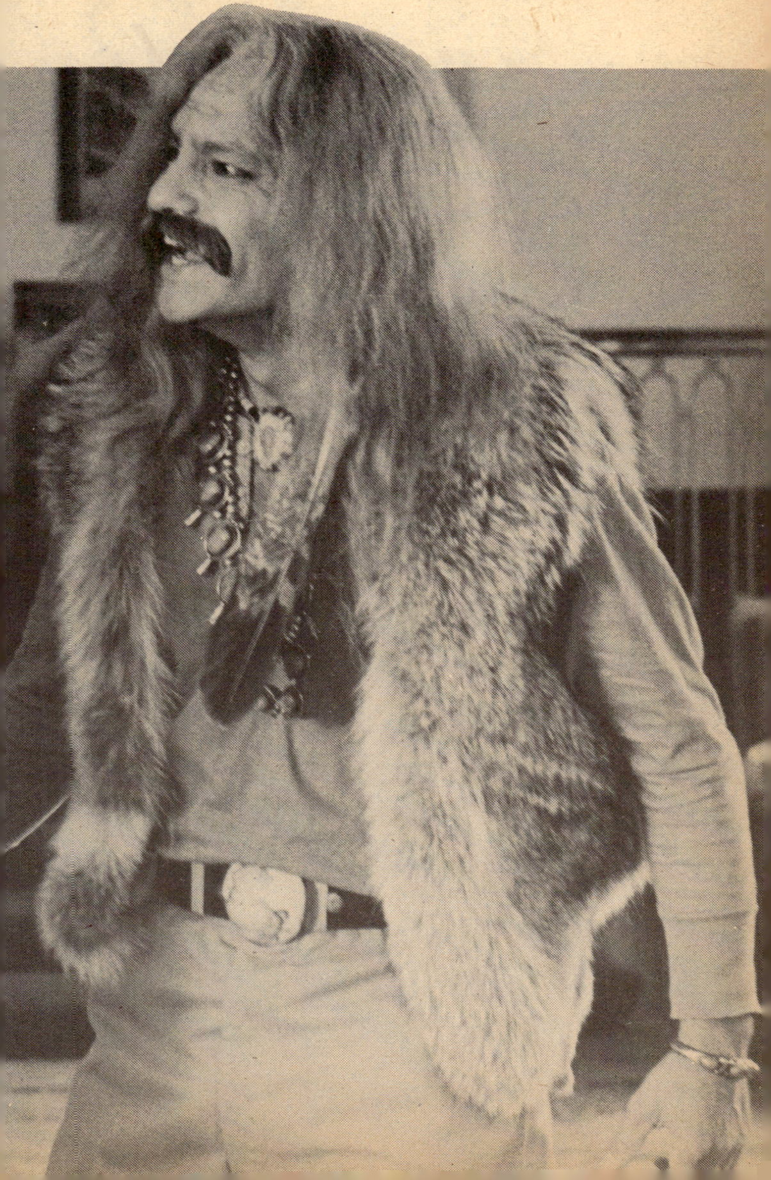

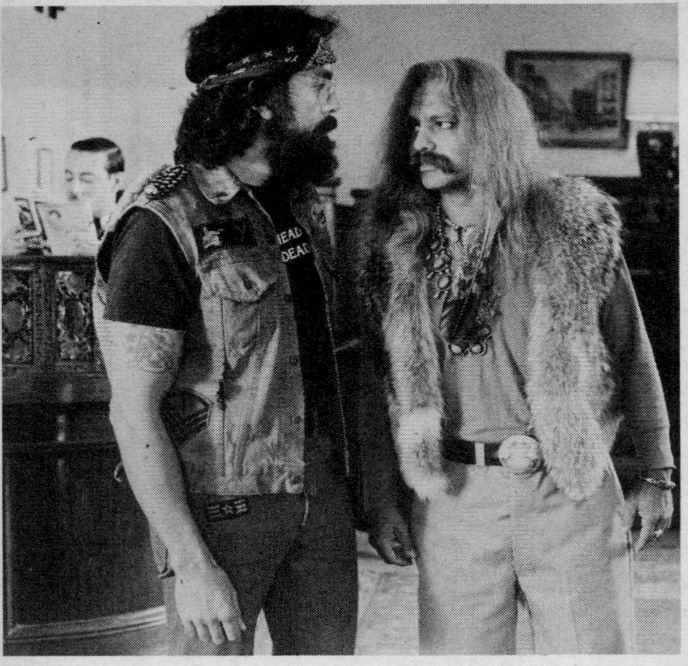

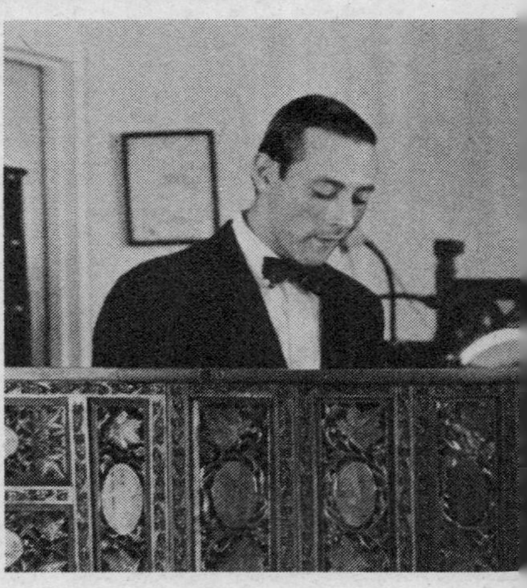

Left: Tommy and Red confer about the way to liberate Red's luggage from his hotel room. It seems there's a little matter of an unpaid bill.

Below: Of course, *first* they try the polite, humble approach. The desk clerk is too busy training his pet cockroaches to pay attention, so . . .

Above: Tommy tries the persuasive method. It's called shaking-the-clerk-until-the-key-falls-out.

Right: Never mess with a desk clerk who has slicked-down hair and a bow tie . . . he just might call the cops!

73

A SURVIVAL TIP

It's not generally known but fire escapes can also be used to **enter** a room as well as to leave it. Sometimes though . . .

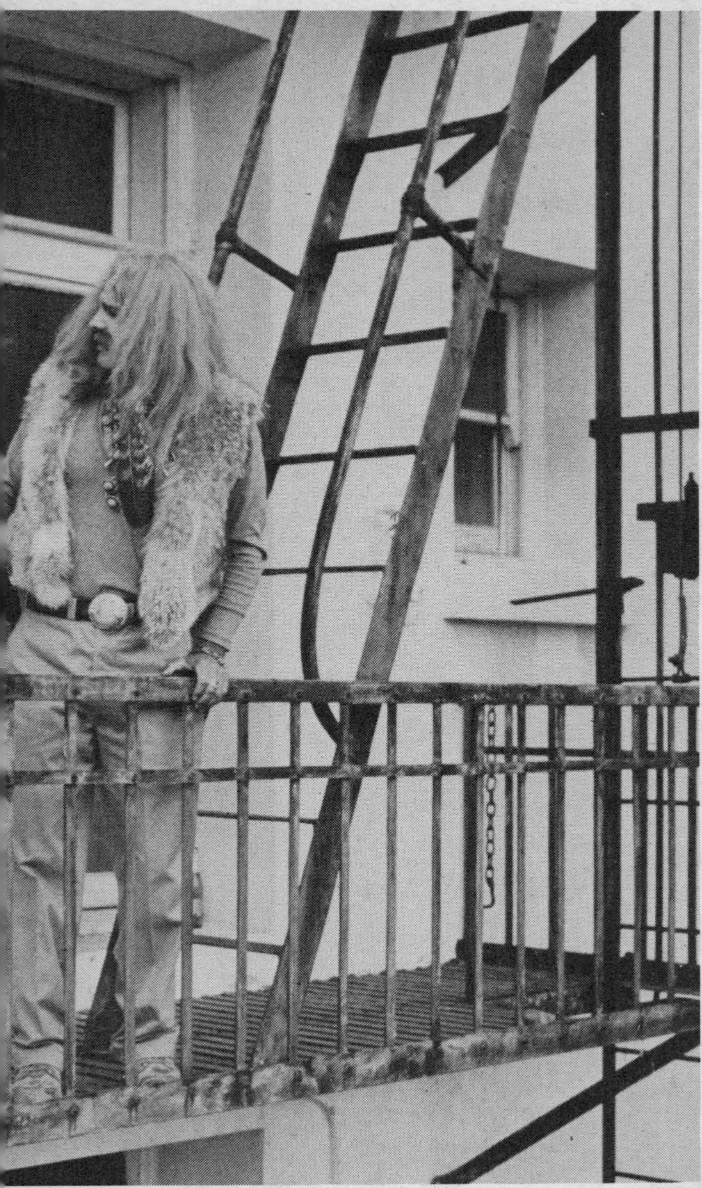

. . . you might find yourself in the wrong room. Better make the best of it!

Wow, Sweetie, did you invite visitors? This is far out!

Yipe!

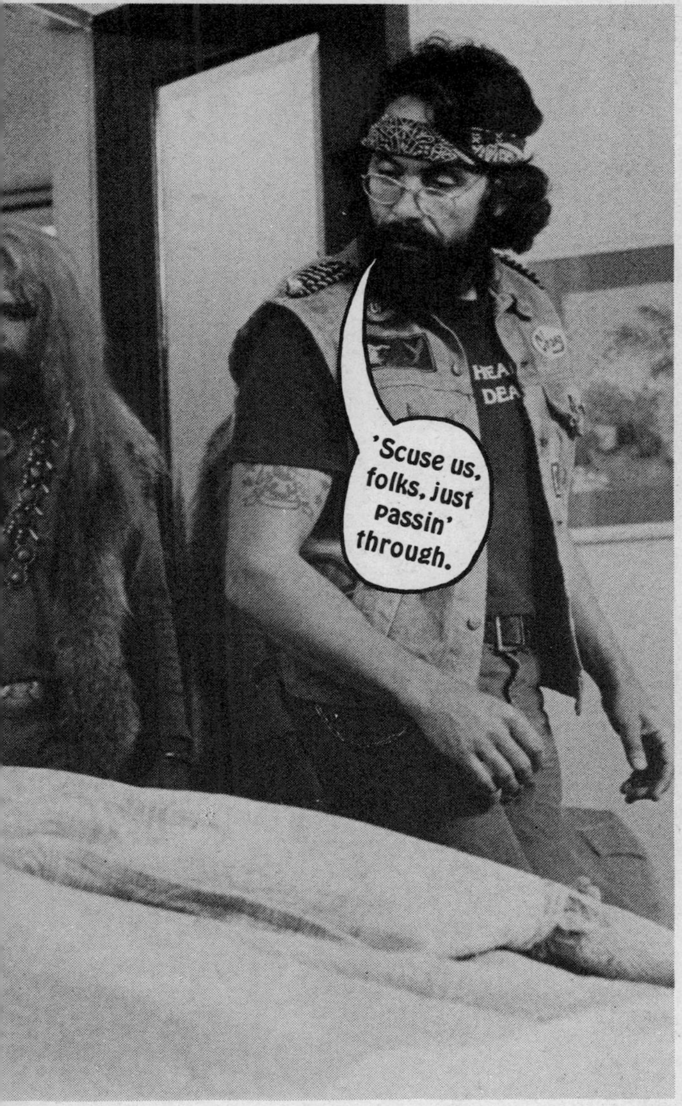
'Scuse us, folks, just passin' through.

Cousin Red's cash crop is examined by a true connoisseur.

The lover's first spat

He wants to call the cops.
She wants to call Tommy and Red back.

A phone call from the hotel brought out the S.W.A.T. team as well as everyone on Hollywood Boulevard.

Okay, you goof-ups, come out with your hands up, your hats off, and looking sober

There's a suspicious-looking character.

Tommy leaves the scene as a policeman grabs the nonplussed desk clerk and then frisks him for contraband.

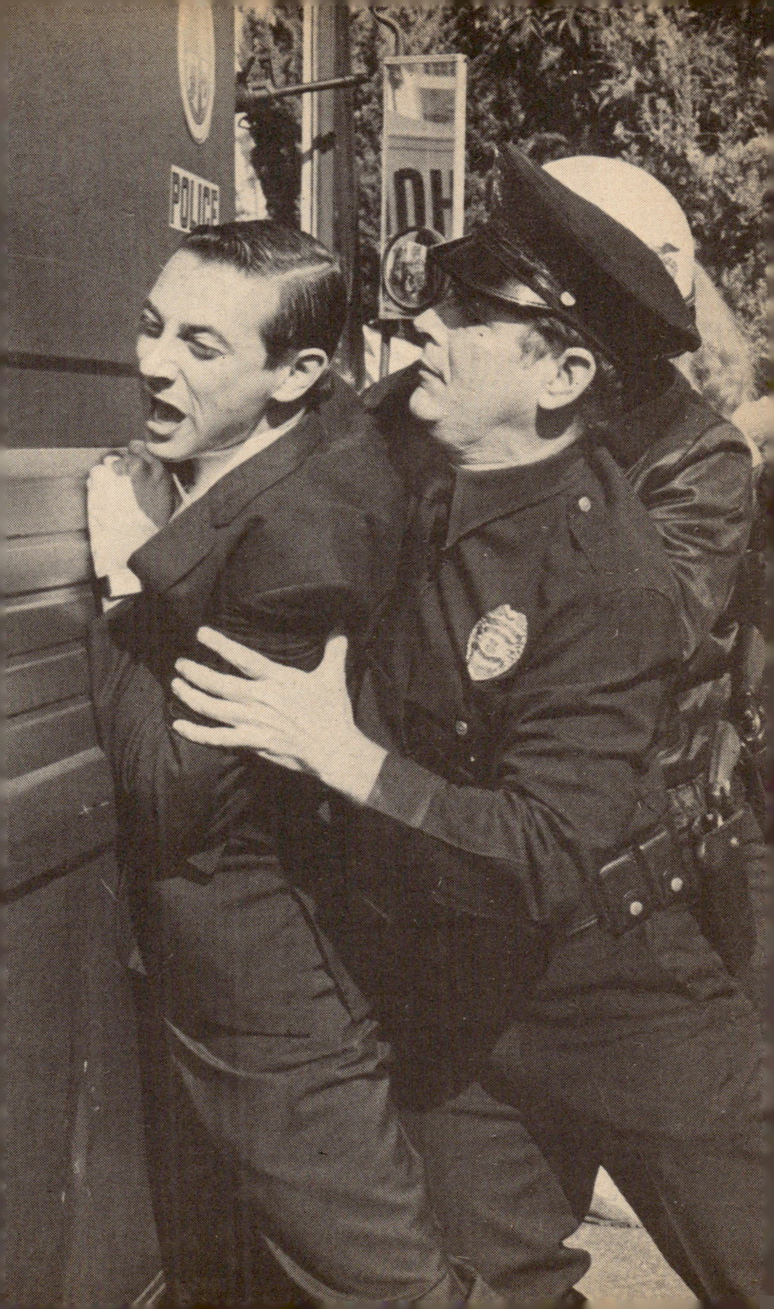
POLICE

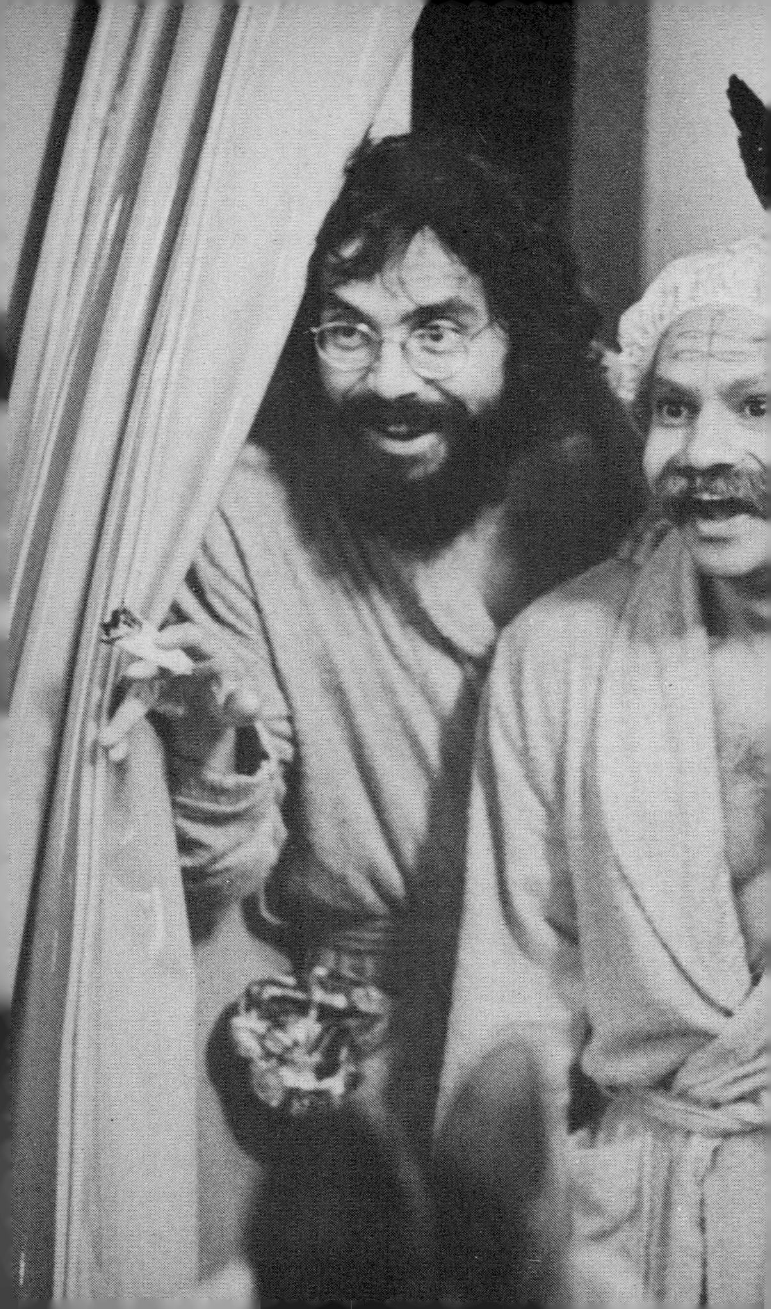

In all the confusion at the hotel, Tommy and Red escape . . . to a nearby massage parlor. Cheech *did* tell Tommy to show his country cousin the sights. . . .

86

Chicken Charlie, one of the massage parlor's best customers, with Candy, his favorite masseuse.

Oh-oh, I think this cluck just laid an egg.

Red decides this would be a fine time to play his cassette recording of S.W.A.T.-team sound effects.

For some strange reason, the massage parlor is instantly cleared. . . .

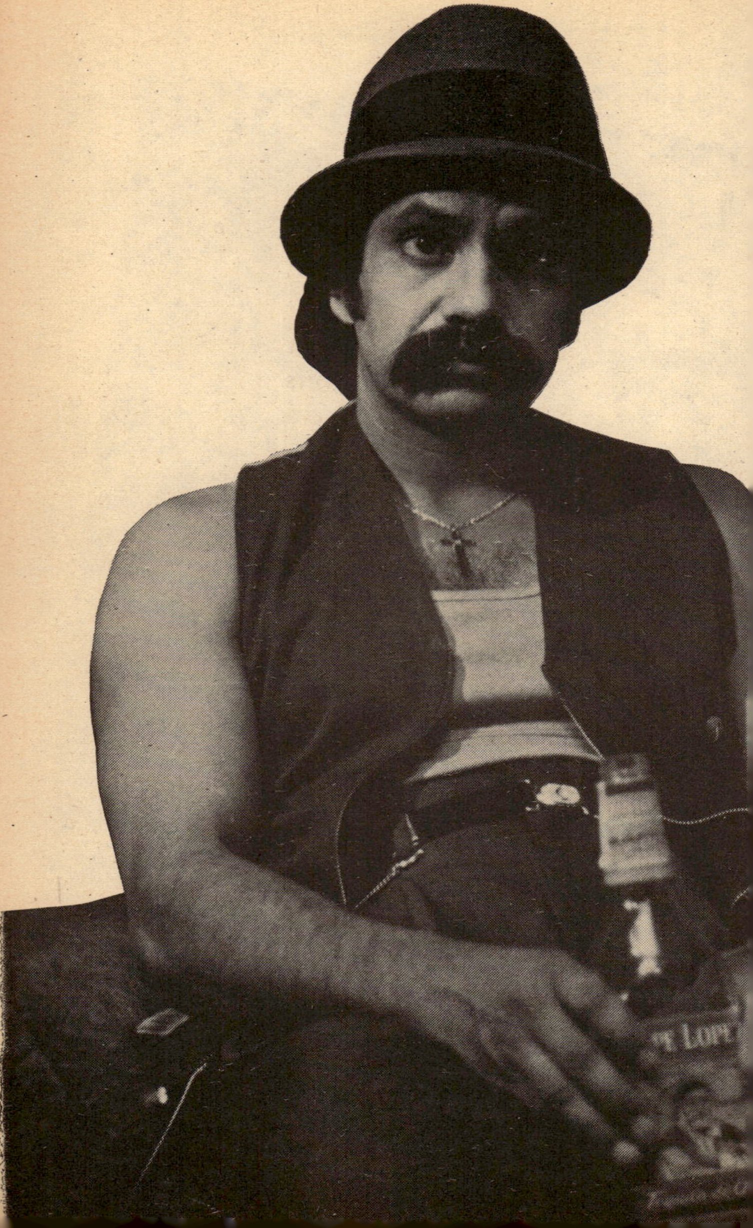

Meanwhile back at the pad, Cheech hits the bottle and watches the TV while waiting for Donna.

Tommy and Red invite Candy the masseuse along for a tour of the town. First stop: the local music store.

Above right: Tommy smokes a fine little number. *Below right:* Red sees a fine little number.

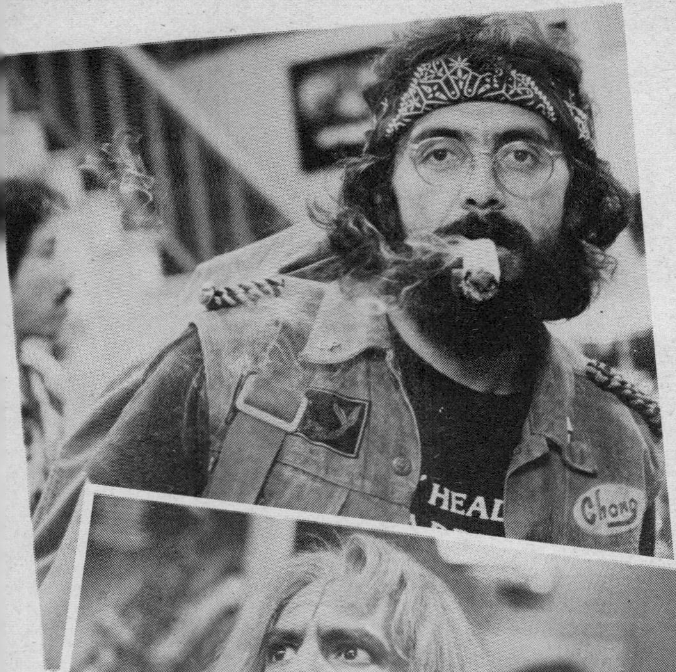
HEAD
Chong

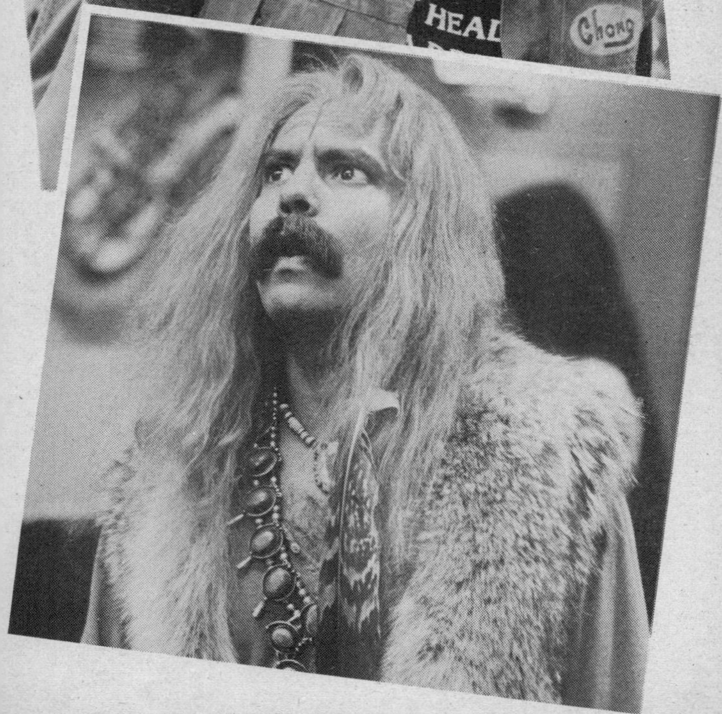

What is the fine little number Cousin Red sees?

Wrong! It's a guitar.

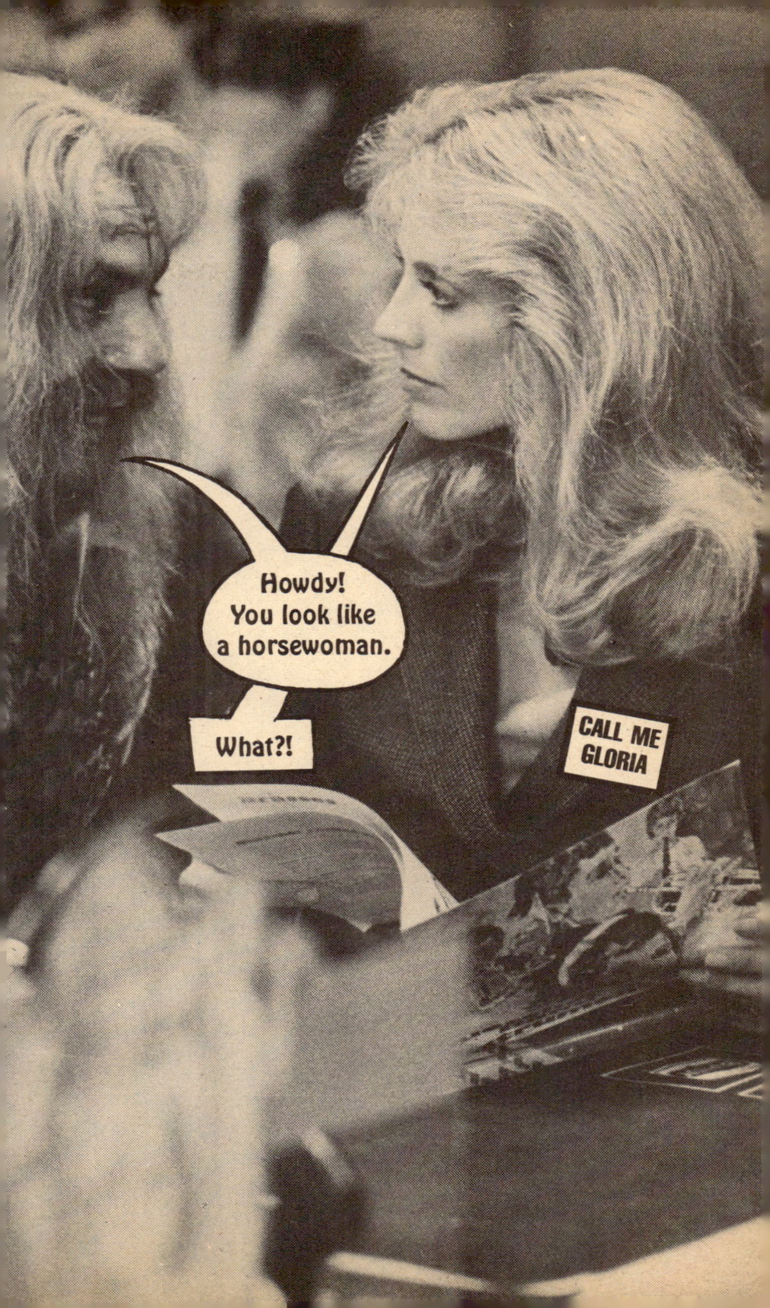
Howdy! You look like a horsewoman.
What?!
CALL ME GLORIA

ONCE TOMMY AND RED START ROCKIN' THERE'S NO STOPPING THEM . . .

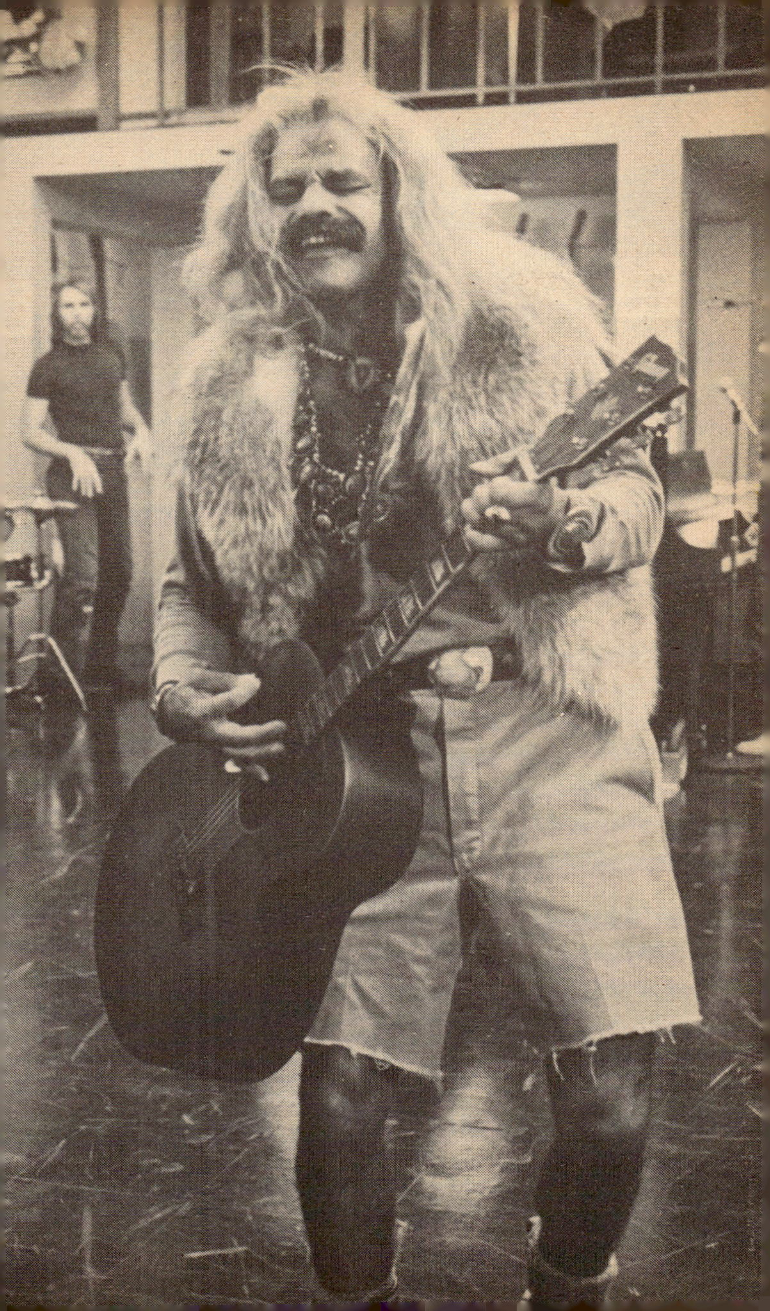

. . . EVEN THOUGH EVERYONE TRIES,

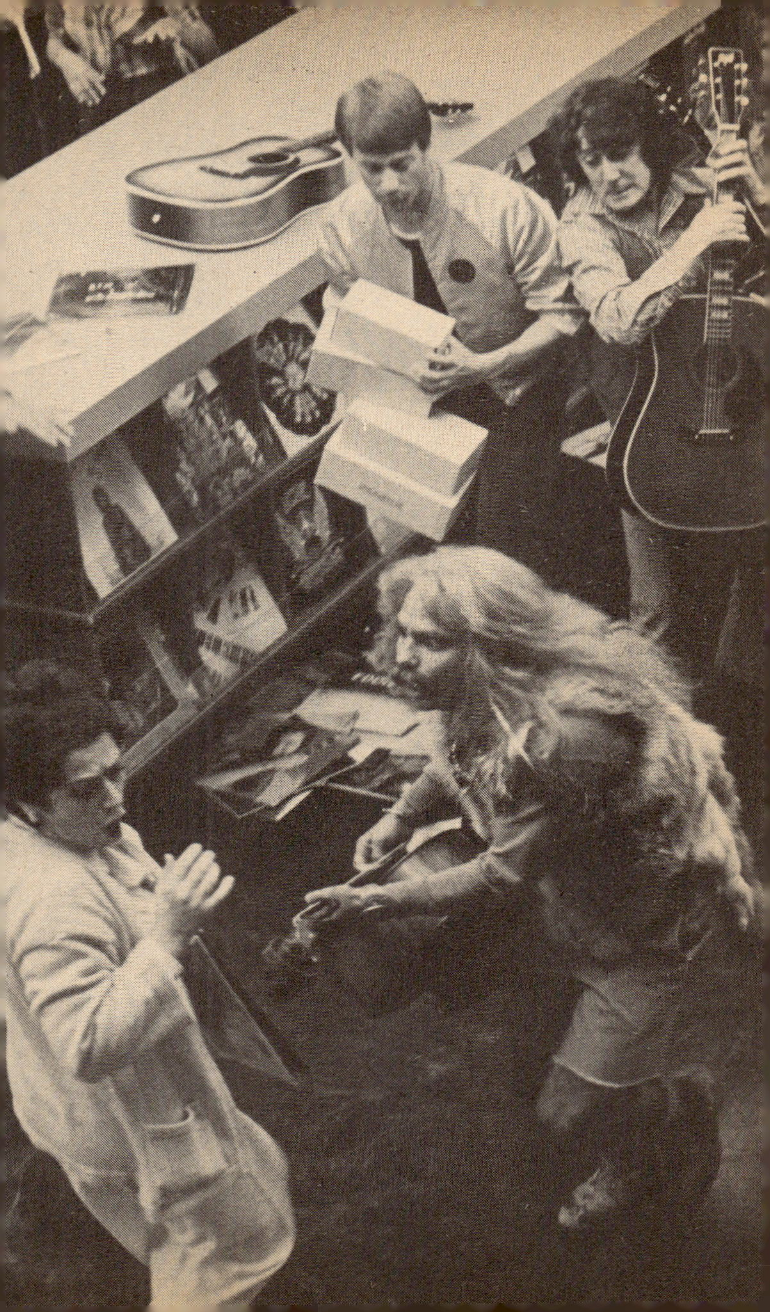

AND TRIES,

AND TRIES,

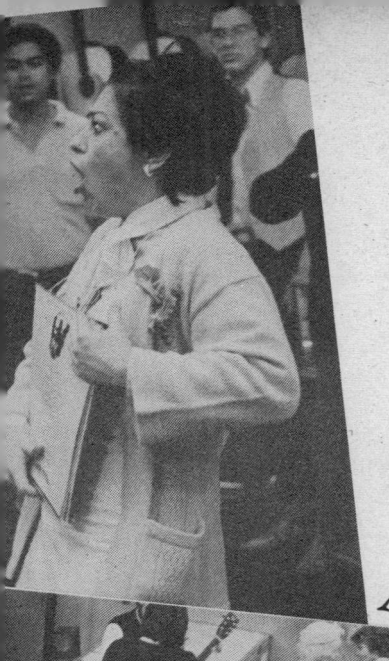

AND TRIES.

But Red's got the jump on them and the unlikely foursome — Tommy, Red, Candy and Gloria — is off to Gloria's house for dinner.

103

Poor Cheech!

He is missing all the fun. He's cleaned the house, ironed everything in sight—including his shoelaces—brushed up on his dance routine, and polished off the Tequila. But Donna is taking her own sweet time getting to his pad.

Here he is bone tired and bleary-eyed from staring at the TV set. If Donna doesn't show up soon, he will be forced to turn it on.

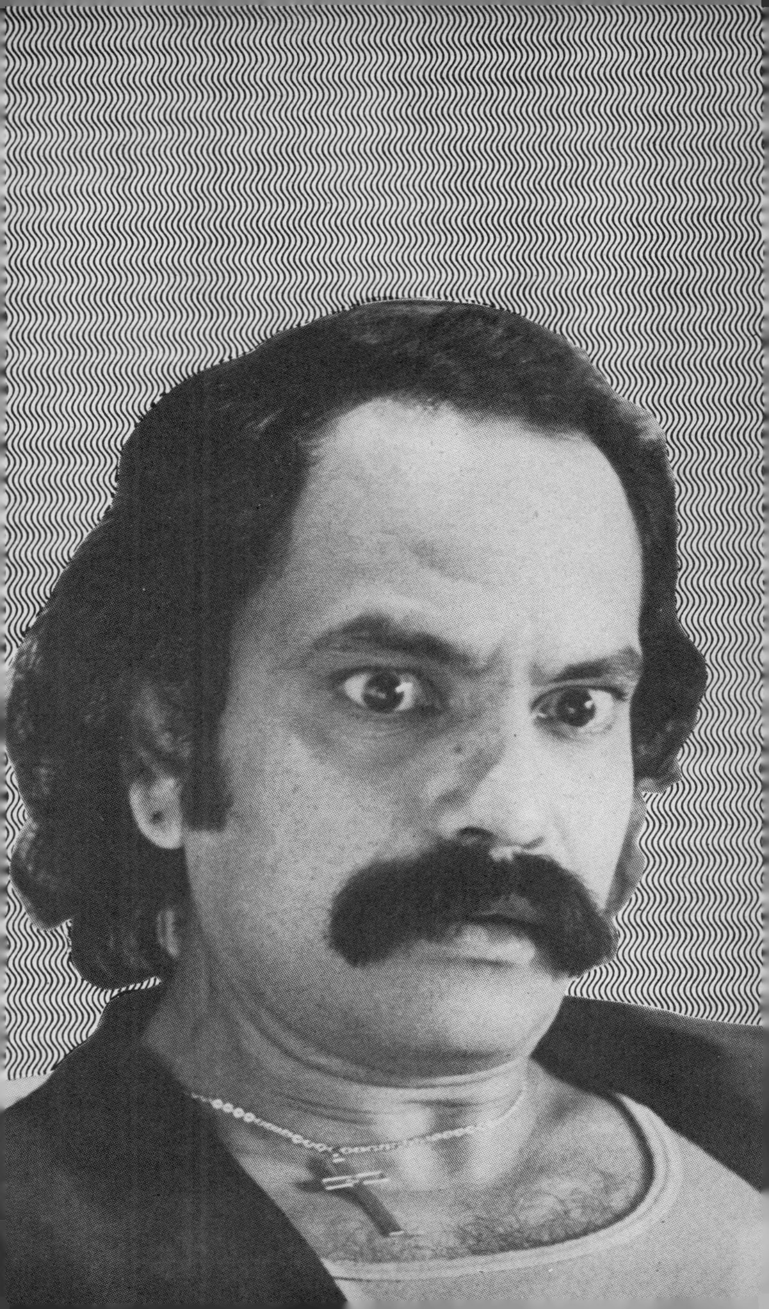

The smile on Red's face is one of surprise. He didn't expect Gloria to live in a mansion.

* * *

The look on the maid's face is one of shock. She thought Halloween was in October.

* * *

You can't see the look on Candy's face (right). She's amazed that even her heels are high.

107

108

Whew! Isn't this fun!
I'll get some treats for you adorable tricksters. . . .

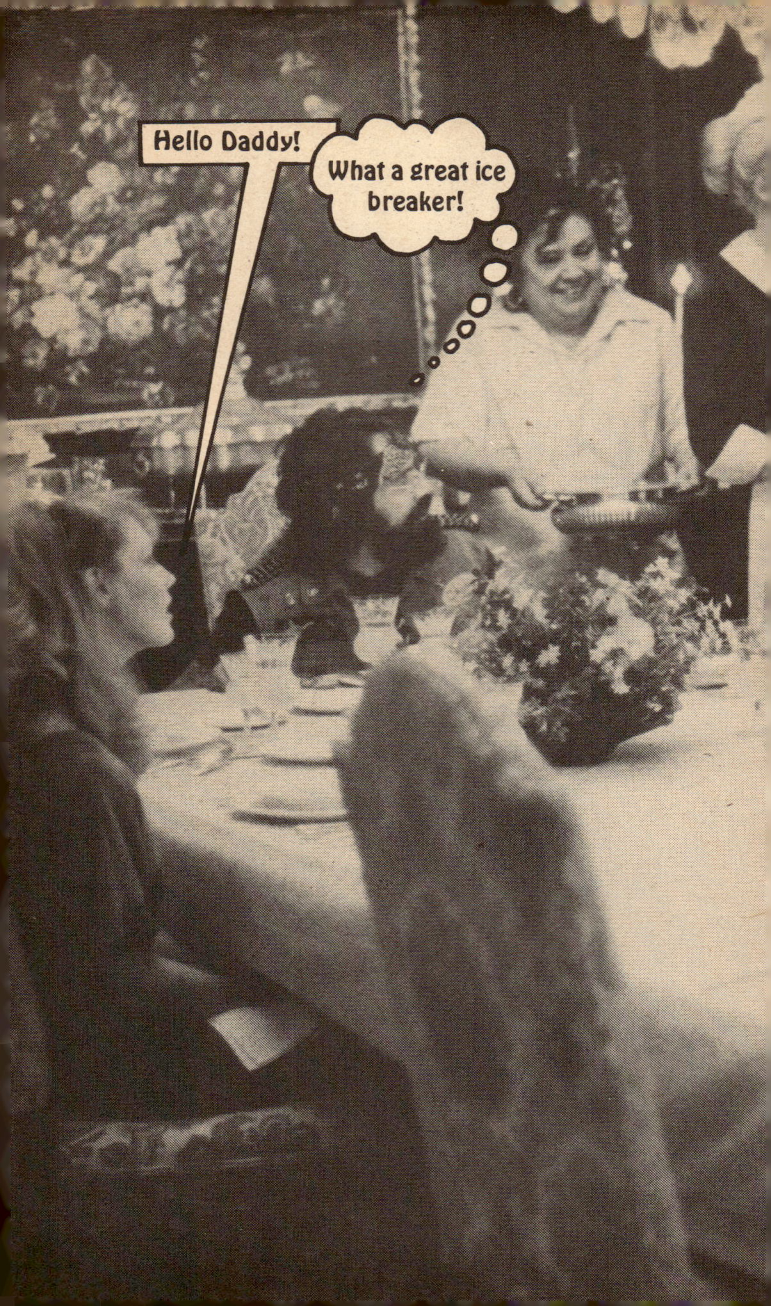
Hello Daddy!
What a great ice breaker!

Oh, mygod. Candy! From the massage parlor!
Look gang! Chicken Charlie is here!

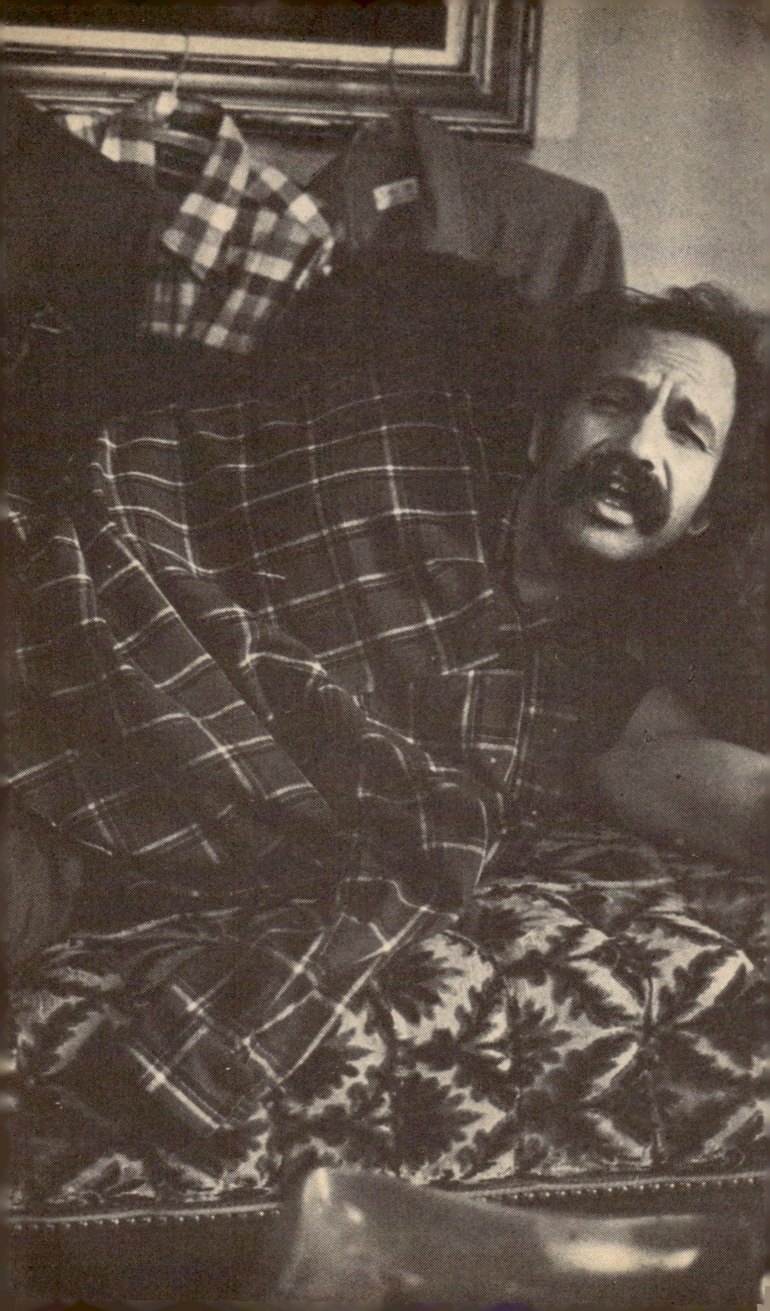

MEANWHILE . . .

Cheech finally turns on the TV set and promptly falls asleep. In his dream, he reaches out for Donna.

THE HAPPY COUPLE

Delicious Donna and Charming Cheech in a dreamy embrace are interrupted by a familiar nightmare. Mr. Neatnick is at it again, complaining about Cheech having fun.

THE UNHAPPY NEIGHBOR

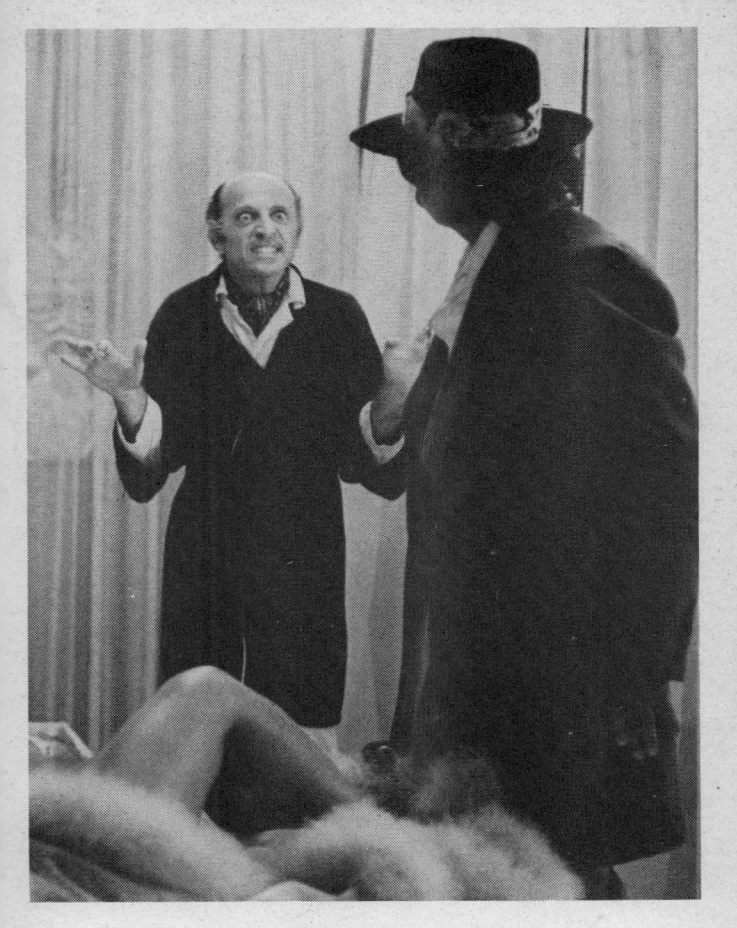

Mr. Neatnick
Don't you people ever sleep?

Cheech
Cool it, man,
you know this is a dream.
Cut out that noise!

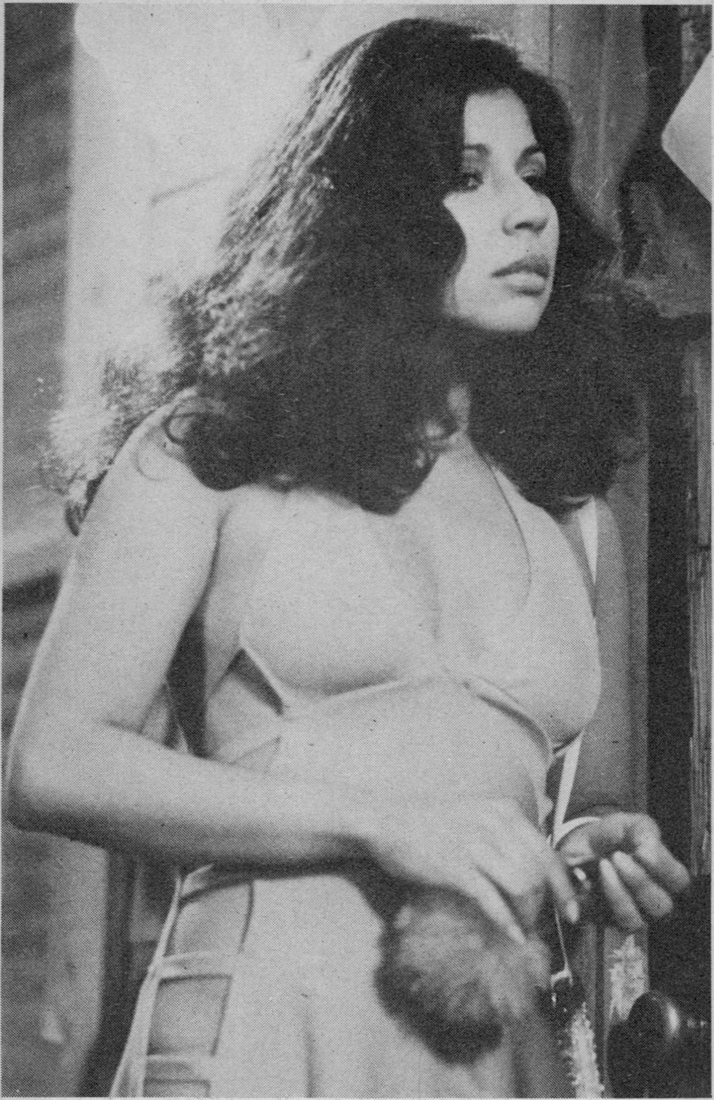

The noise Cheech hears in his dream is not Neatnick, it's Donna. Here she is in the flesh, all dressed (?) up, knocking on his door. But Cheech sleeps on, and Donna storms off.

Welfare my foot! Wait 'till he comes around for more social service.

After dinner, Tommy and Red return the hospitality by commandeering the family Rolls to take Gloria and her folks to The Comedy House, a local nightclub where anybody can be a star.

The smoke from Tommy's giant joint gets everyone stoned. Red makes a spectacle of himself and Gloria's mother eggs him on.

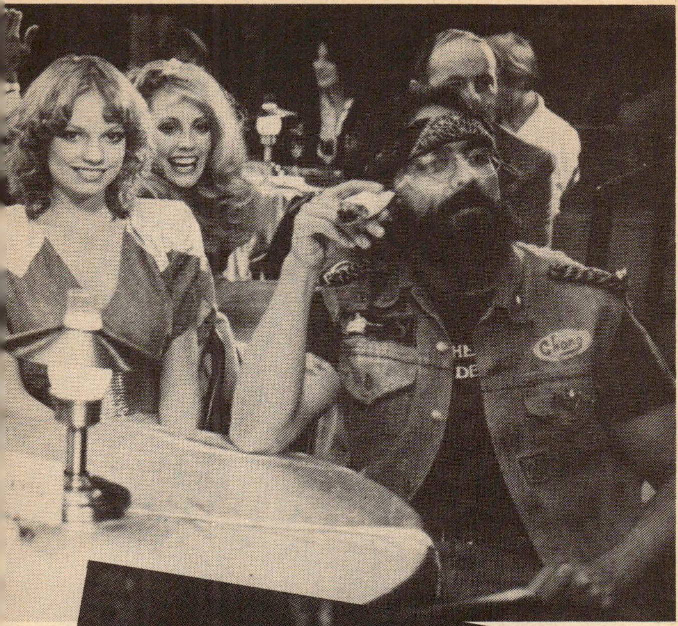
Chong

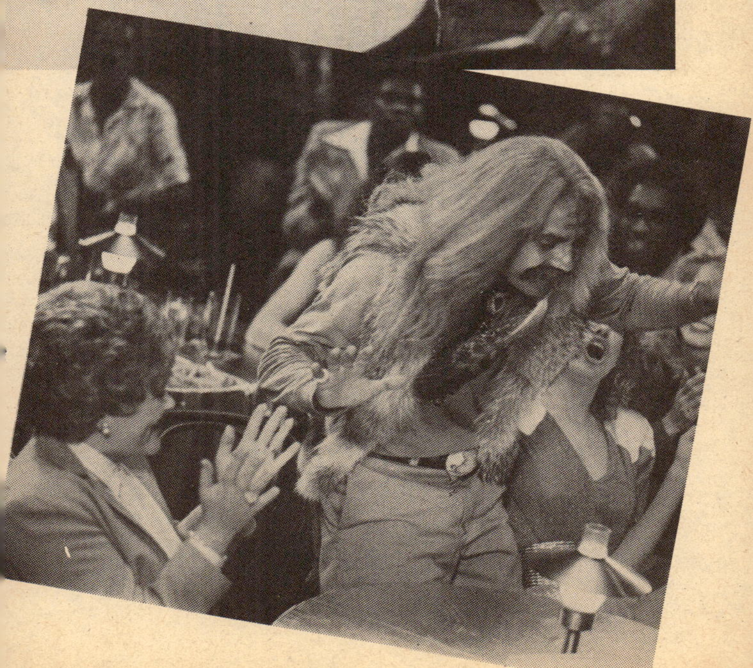

This is really hilarious . . .

Do you read shorthand?
Short . . . Hand! Get it?

This couple's in a car, and she says, "Watch the road." Then he says, "Why, is it going anywhere?"

. . . Thud!

RED'S ACT

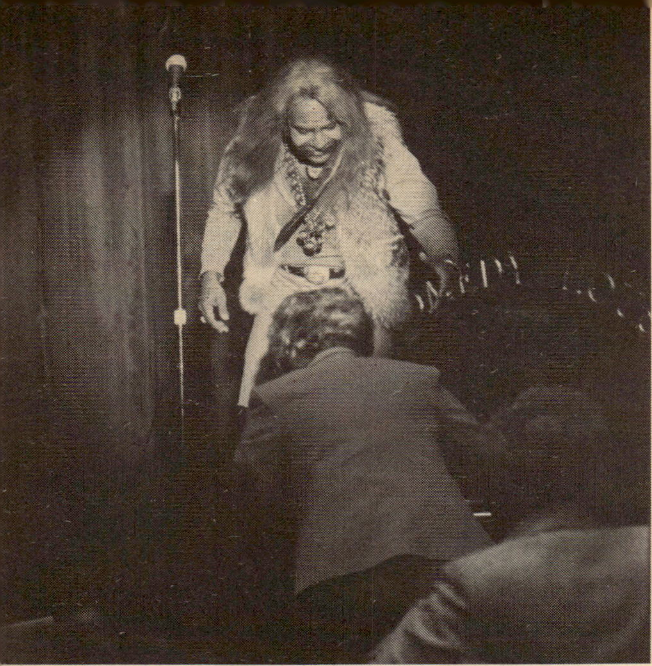

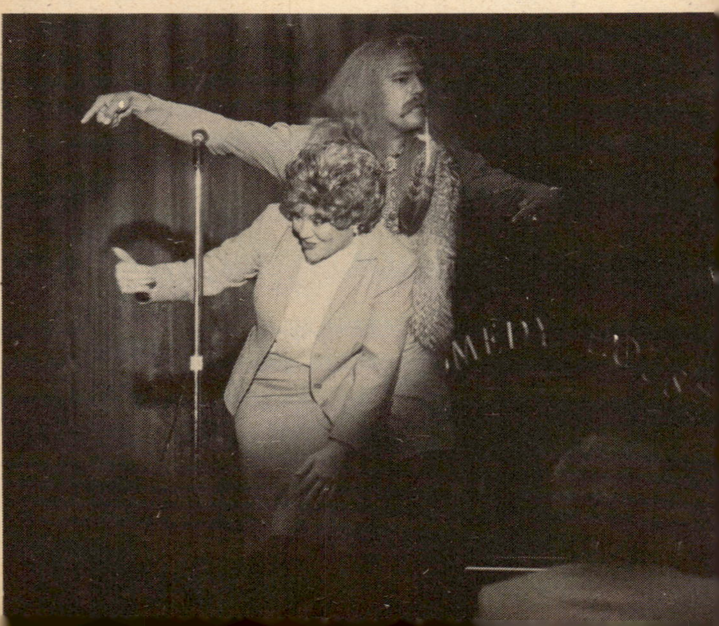

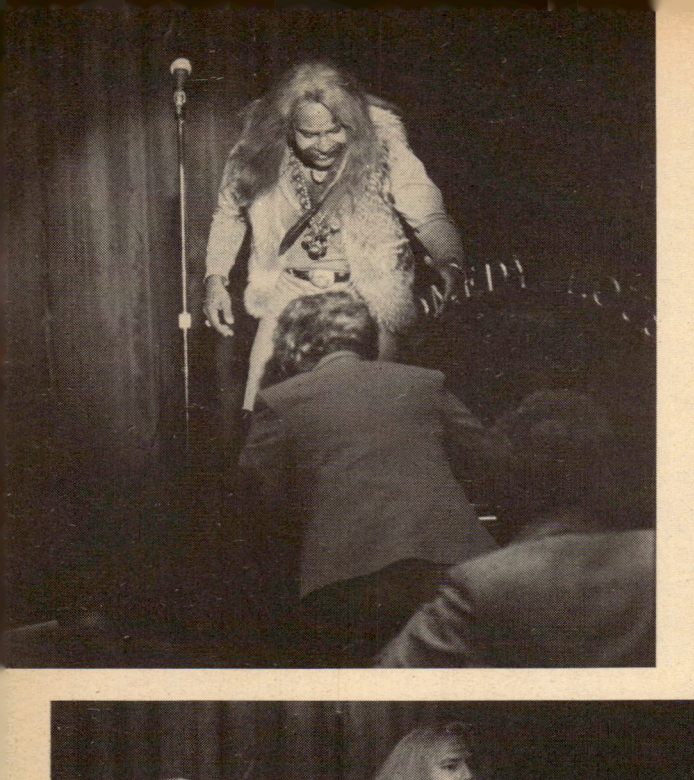

By popular demand, Red does not do an encore. Instead, Tommy comes up to tell his famous "Piece of Fruit" joke, which so breaks up Gloria's mother that she's unable to stop laughing and the management is about to take drastic measures.

> Isn't this peachy?

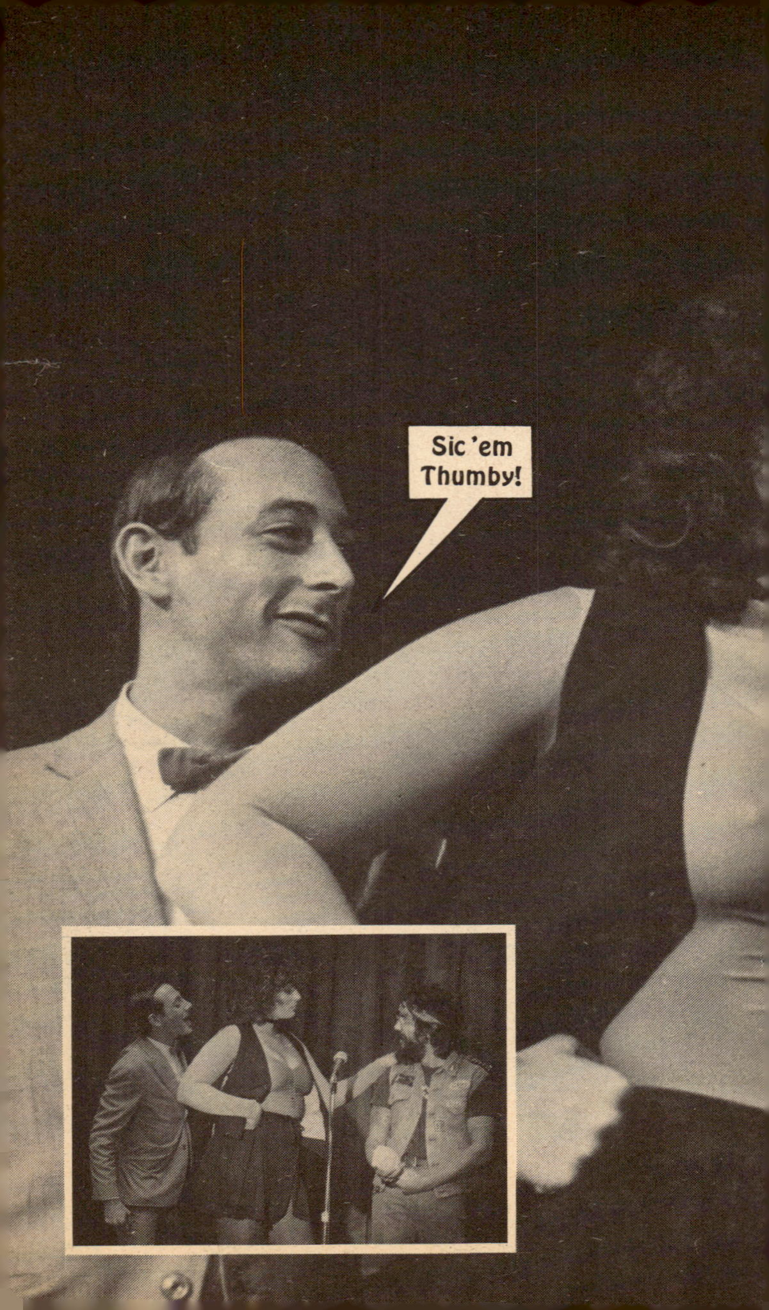
Sic 'em Thumby!

It's Thumbelina, The Comedy House's bouncer... and guess who's with her? Right! The crazed hotel clerk out to get Tommy.

Isn't it strange that riots seem to break out wherever these two go?

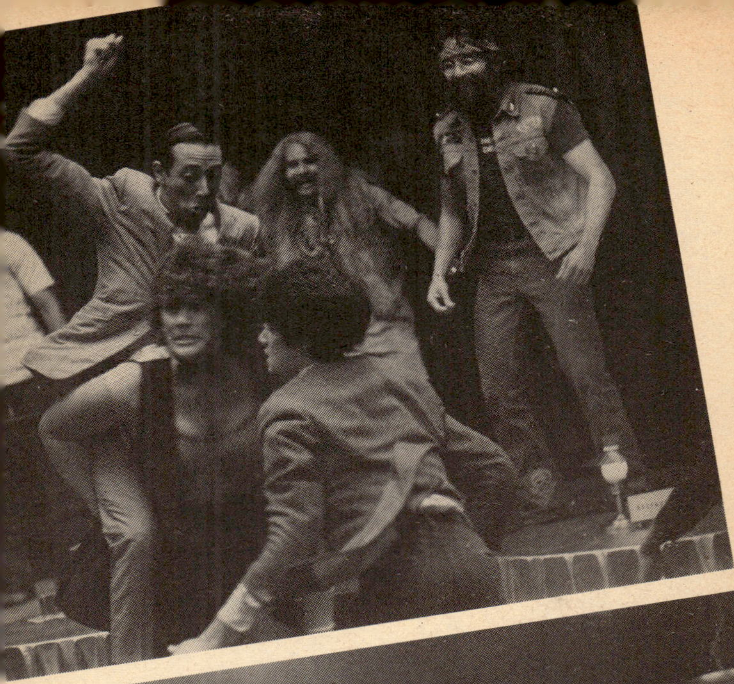

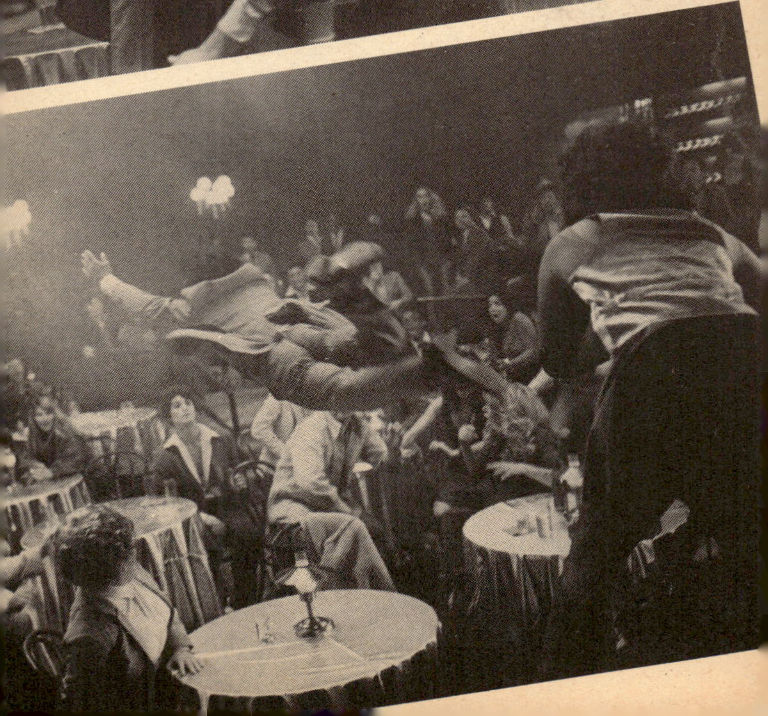

Tommy and Red escape the melee by leaping into a Ferrari at the valet parking entrance. They wind up at Red's marijuana farm with the cops on their trail. Suddenly, something lights the sky, and they are pulled up into space.

HOLY SPACESHIP!

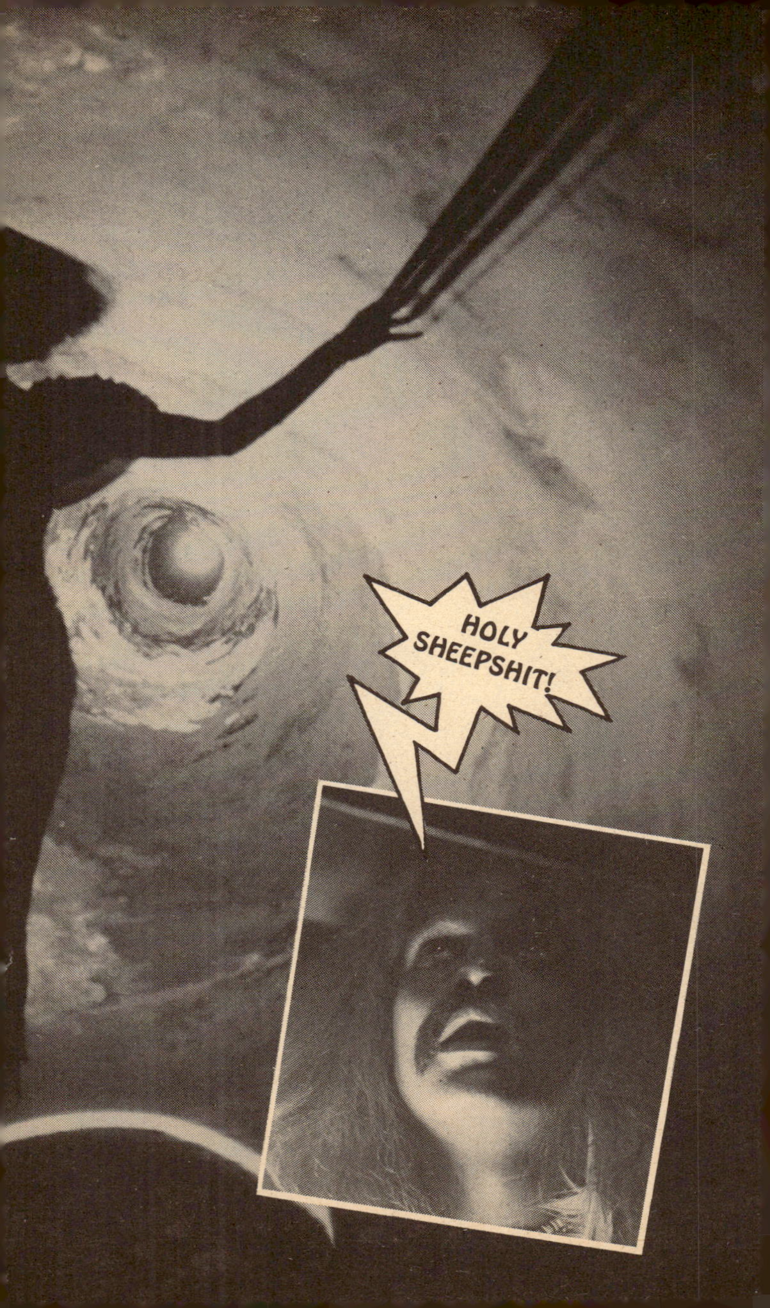
HOLY SHEEPSHIT!

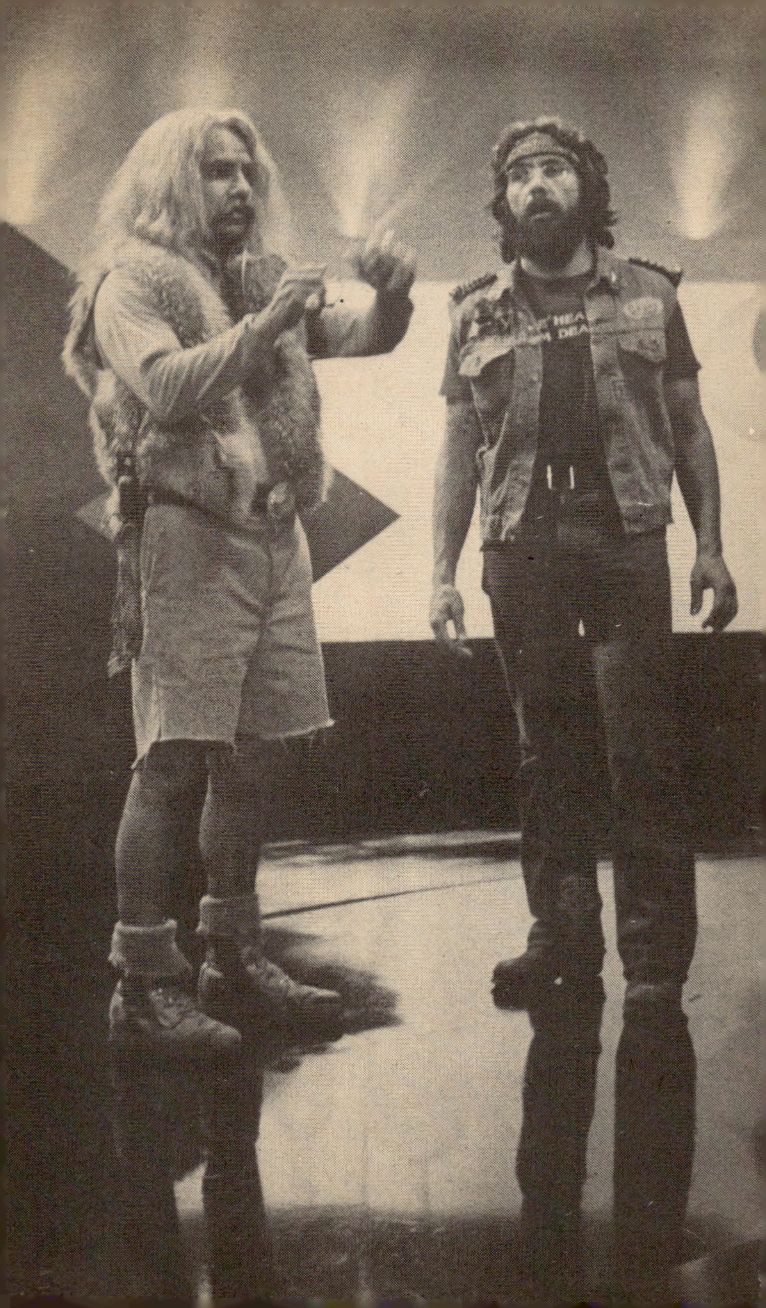

Red and Tommy find
themselves in a spaceship.
Not just any spaceship,
but a pot-powered one!
They sniff in wonder at
their good fortune.

> Look man, dig this....

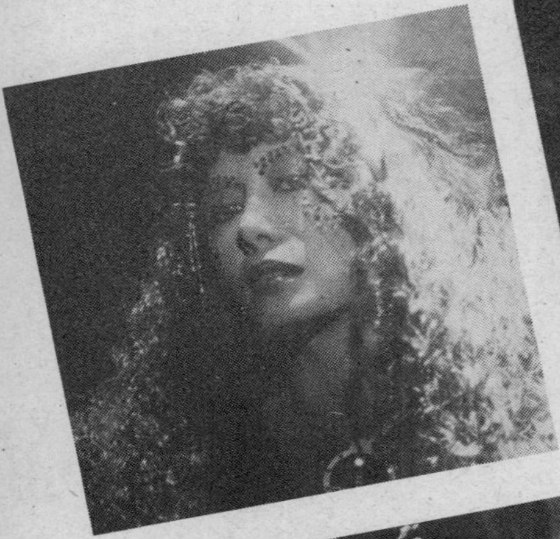
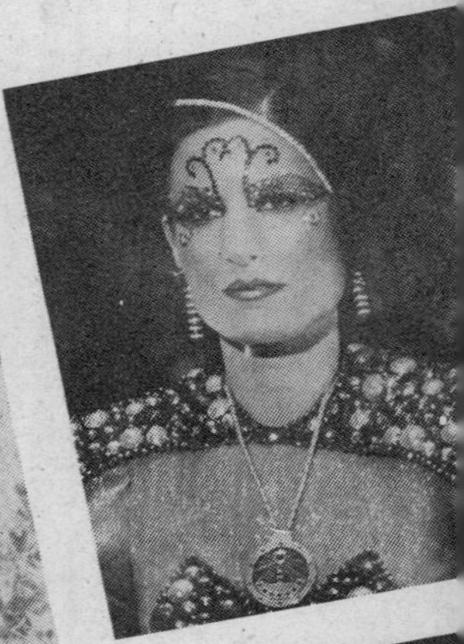
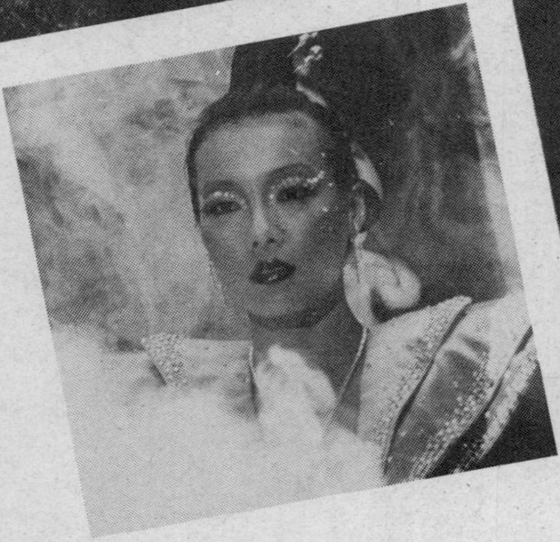
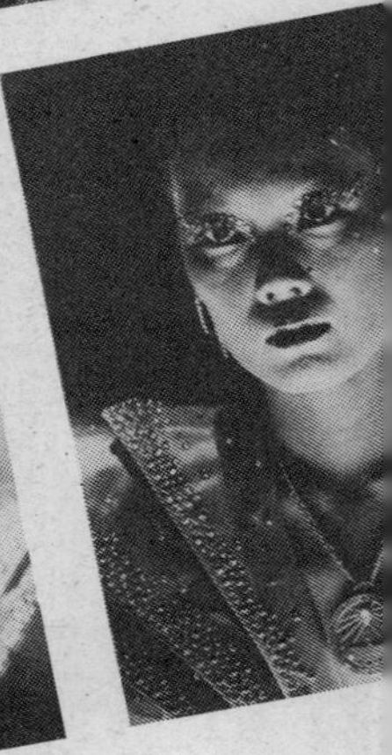

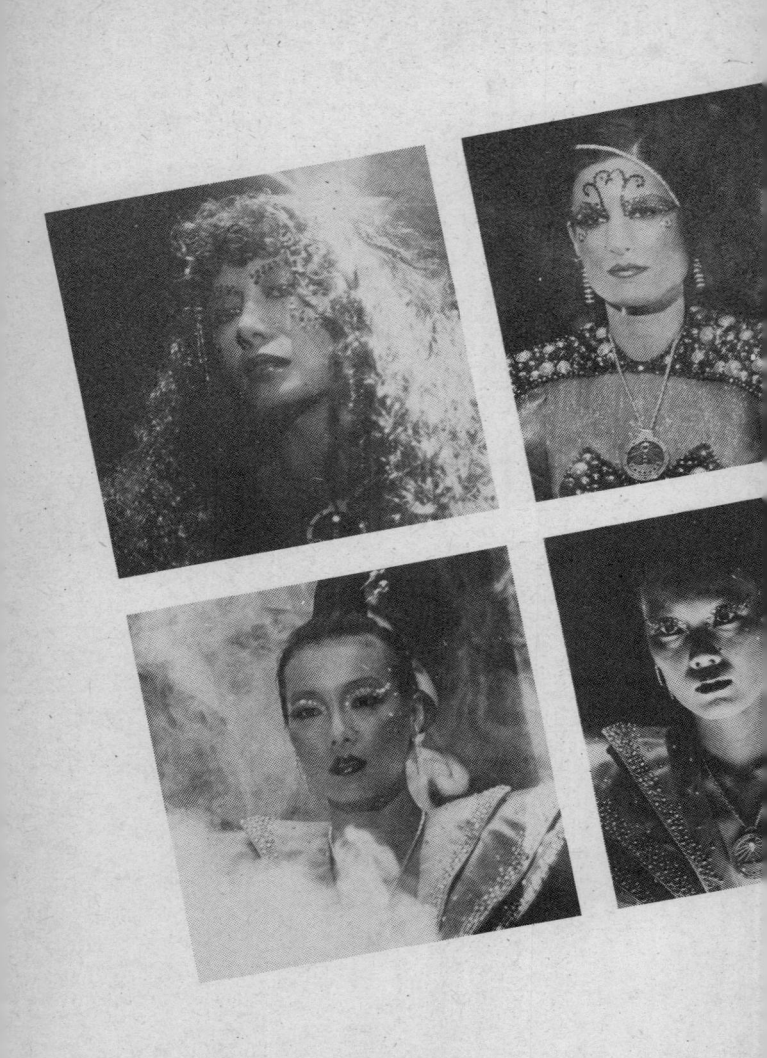

There are the magnificent astronettes, whose mission is to find replacements for the men on their planet who are wearing out. The first thing they must do is . . .

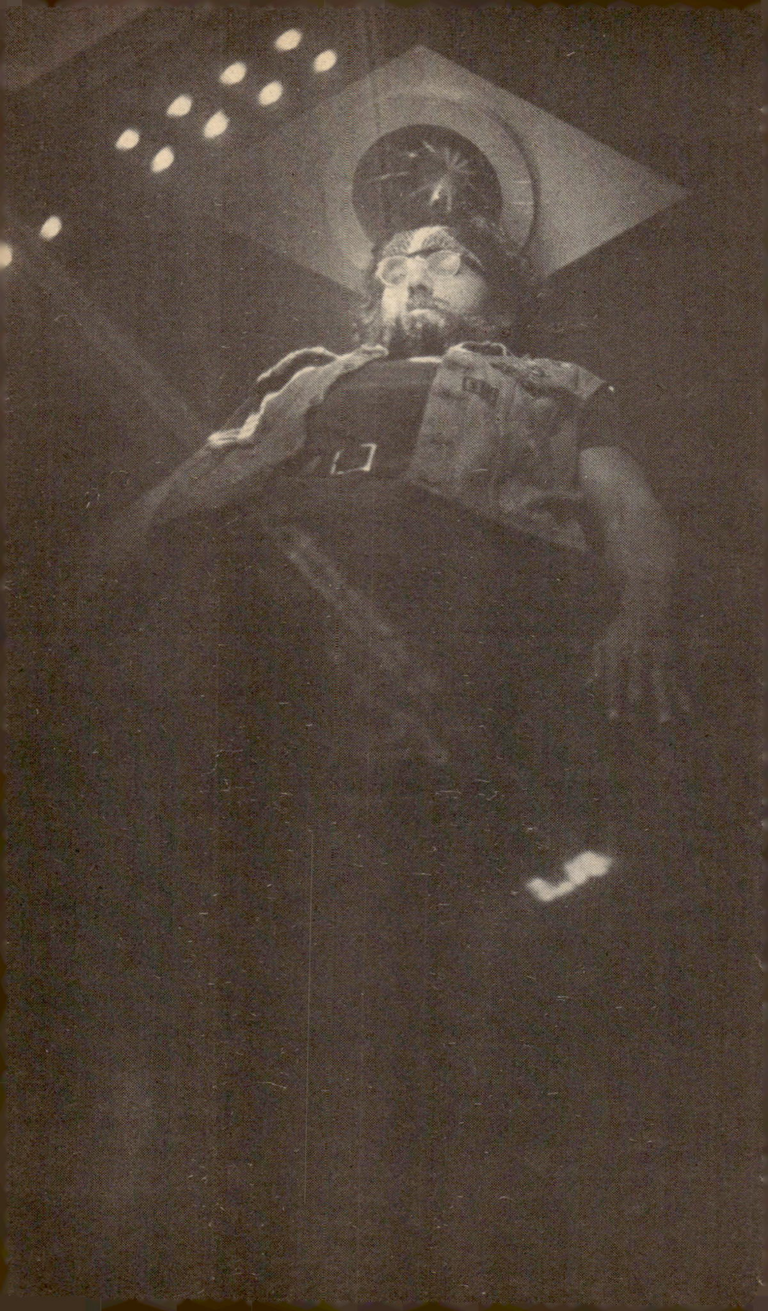

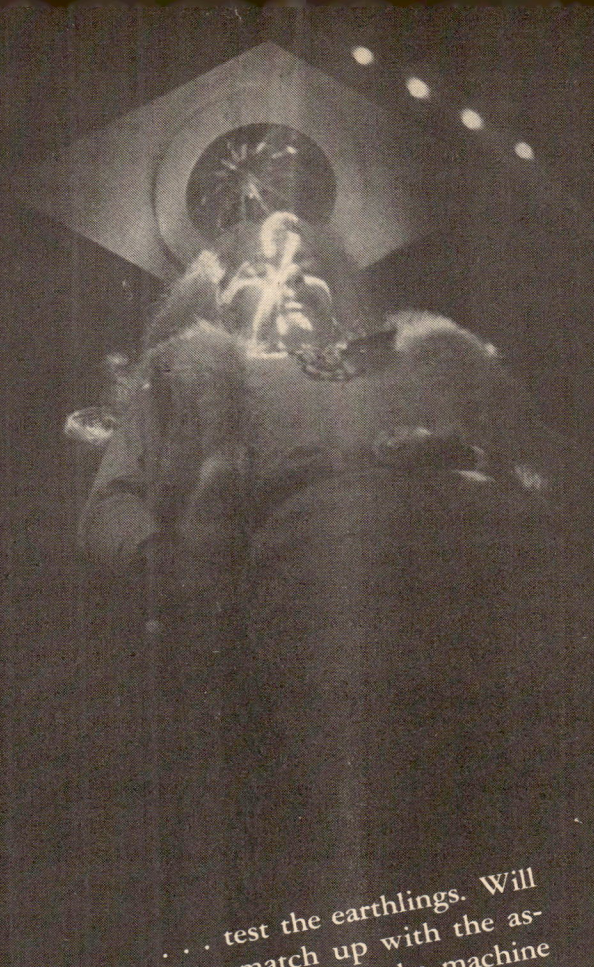

. . . test the earthlings. Will they match up with the astronettes? Only the machine will tell.

136

Meanwhile, back on earth, Cheech keeps dreaming. This time he is an Aztec prince offering his princess Donna to the gods.

"Send me a sign, man."

But the only thing in the heavens is that far out spaceship. Red and Tommy emerge from the machine transformed—at least outwardly. Note their new outfits.

Holy sheepshit, I'm staying here. I ain't going back nohow!

This is not for me. I got to get back. I've got important things to do.

SUDDENLY TOMMY IS HOME.

Hey Cheech, wake up! Wake up man! You'll feel better when you get a whiff of some of this space dust. It's out of this world....

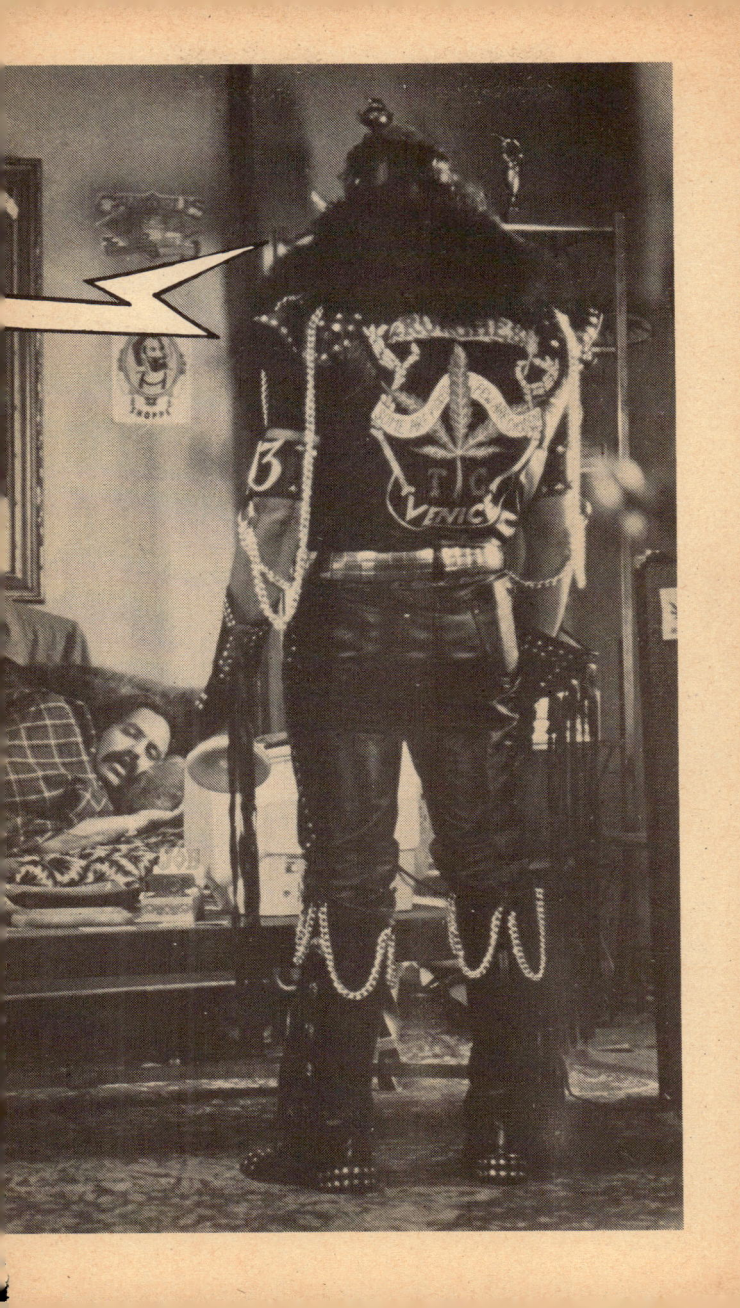

UNIVERSAL PICTURES PRESENTS
C&C BROWN PRODUCTIONS, INC.

CHEECH AND CHONG

IN

CHEECH AND CHONG'S NEXT MOVIE

WRITTEN BY THOMAS CHONG & CHEECH MARIN
ASSOCIATE PRODUCER PETER MACGREGOR-SCOTT
PRODUCED BY HOWARD BROWN
DIRECTED BY THOMAS CHONG

Cast of Characters

Cheech	RICHARD MARIN
Chong	THOMAS CHONG
Donna	EVELYN GUERRERO
Candy	BETTY KENNEDY
Mr. Neatnik	SY KRAMER
Gloria	RIKKI MARIN
Chicken Charlie	BOB McCLURG
Gloria's Mother	EDIE McCLURG
Pee Wee Herman/Desk Clerk	PAUL REUBENS
Gay Motorcyclist	PETER BROMILOW
Executive	PAUL "MOUSIE" GARNER
Massage Girl	NAN MASON
Music Store Salesman	JONATHAN T. MOORE
Old Lady	LUPE M. ONTIVEROS
Cop Shotgun	ED PECK
Miss Hatchet	MARGUERITE RAY
Drunk in Welfare Office	JOHN STEADMAN
Bulk	JAKE STEINFELD
Gas Station Owner	ROBERT ACKERMAN
Doorman	BOBBY A.
Welfare Child	LITA AUBRY
Second Assistant Director	GARY AUSTIN
Cop Driver	JONNIE BARNETT
Man in Hotel	DON BOVINGLOH
Woman in Hotel	PHYLLIS KATZ
Beautiful	SHELBY CHONG
Swedish Maid	CAROLYN CONWELL
Cameraman	DOUG COX
One Man Band	DON DAVIS
Massage Parlor Owner	BOB DREW
Grandma in Music Store	MAXINE ELLIOTT
First Assistant Director	DICK FRATTALI
Cook	MARGARITA GARCIA

Welfare Actor	MARK H. GILMAN
Chick Hazard—Private Eye	PHIL HARTMAN
Wardrobe Girl	KIM S. HOPKINS
Bad Guy—El Pachuco	STEVEN KAVNER
Wino	ROBERT LINDER
Kid in Street	PARIS CHONG
Leaflet Lady	SUSAN MECHSNER
Third Assistant Director	TRACY NEWMAN
Director	JOHN PARAGON
Guard at Gate #1	FRANK PICARD
Loud Mouth Black	BEN POWERS
Robot	PETER RISCH
Mexican Man in Welfare Office	NATIVIDAD VACIO
Junkie in Welfare Office	TONY VISCARRA
Loud Mouth Black	MICHAEL WINSLOW
Johnny	MARCUS WYATT
Pinochle Players	ALVIN CHILDRESS
	DeFOREST COVAN
Massage Girls	AMANDA CLEVELAND
	GAY GULDSTRAND
	CHRISTINE A. McKEE
	BRANDY ROE
	VICTORIA WELLS
Clients	JOHN PETLOCK
	DAN CALDWELL
Hostages	RITA WILSON
	CATHERINE BERGSTROM
	CASSANDRA PETERSON
Cops at Hotel	PETER GRIFFIN
	TIM CULBERTSON
	CHARLES D. LAIRD
	PAUL E. LEWIS
	CARL WEINTRAUB
Welfare Recipient	MALCOLM DRUMMOND
Lady Bouncer	FAITH MINTON
Startled Man	RUBEN GUEVARA
Standup Comic	TIM SILVA
Space Girls	RAE DAWN CHONG
	PAMELA FONG
	CASSANDRA GAVIOLA
	SHIRLEE KONG
	LINDA REDFORD
	LEE SCANLON
	MAILE SOUZA
	PRECIOUS CHONG
	ROBBI CHONG
Stunts	GEORGE SAWAYA
	RICK SAWAYA
	CINDY WILLS
Director of Photography	KING BAGGOT
Edited by	SCOTT CONRAD, A.C.E.
Production Designer	FRED HARPMAN

Costume Designer	JOE I. TOMPKINS
Special Visual Effects by	ALBERT WHITLOCK
Original Music Performed by	KILLER
Lyrics by	ROCHELLE RUNNELLS
Original Music by	MARK DAVIS
Production Manager	PETER MACGREGOR-SCOTT
First Assistant Director	NEWTON ARNOLD
Second Assistant Director	BOB DOHERTY
Assistant to Producer	BRAD WAISBREN
Production Associate	DOW GRIFFITH
Matte Photography by	BILL TAYLOR
Camera Operator	NICK McLEAN
Assistant Camera	RICHARD WALDEN
Film Editor	TOM AVILDSON
Assistant Film Editor	ROGER GREENE
Special Laser Effects by	LASER MEDIA, INC.
Laser Consultant	LINDA LIVINGSTON
Script Supervisor	MARSHALL SCHLOM
Stunt Coordinator	EDDIE HICE
Casting by	FERN CHAMPION
	and PAMELA BASKER
Make-Up	JERRY O'DELL
Hair Stylist	BARBARA LORENZ
Costume Supervisors	BRUCE ERICKSON
	APRIL FERRY
Set Decorations	BOB BENTON
Sound	DARIN KNIGHT
Sound Re-Recording	BILL McCAUGHEY
	BOB HARMAN
Sound Effects Editor	GIL MARCHANT
Loop Dialogue Editor	JACK GOSDEN
Music Editor	JOHN CAPER, JR.
Animation Designer	FRANK ANDRINA
Animators	ARTHUR FILLOY
	FELICE FORTE
	DUNCAN MARJORIBANKS
	TOBY
	KIRK ANDERSON
	BILL WRAY
	LEONARD JOHNSON
	ALLAN WADE
Property Master	DENNIS PARRISH
Gaffer	GARY HOLT
Key Grip	MARLIN HALL
Transportation Captain	TOM BATTAGLIA
Special Effects	JOE GOSS
Space Ship Optical Effects	MODERN FILM EFFECTS
Space Ship Miniatures	UNIVERSAL HARTLAND
Title & Optical Effects	UNIVERSAL TITLE

PANAFLEX LENSES AND CAMERA BY PANAVISION
COLOR BY TECHNICOLOR